THE CENTRAL TRUTH

UNIVERSITY OF TORONTO DEPARTMENT OF ENGLISH

Studies and Texts, No. 11

THE
CENTRAL TRUTH

The Incarnation in
Robert Browning's Poetry

WILLIAM WHITLA

Well, is the thing we see, salvation?
                                                I
Put no such dreadful question to myself,
Within whose circle of experience burns
The central truth, Power, Wisdom, Goodness,—God.

(*The Ring and the Book*, X, 1630–3)

UNIVERSITY OF TORONTO PRESS

PREFACE

BROWNING'S POETRY, in the words of Dryden's judgment on his age in 1700, is "all, all of a piece throughout." But if the work of a major poet is a unity from first to last, continuing and expanding and re-exploring the same themes and interests, the same subjects, problems, and solutions, it is only rarely, and only in the greatest creative activity, that the wholeness of the poet's universe is visible. Browning is such a poet. He examines many themes and subjects; he presents gallery after gallery of compelling portraiture, and still at the end of his life he finds the same burning fascination in the same themes, subjects, and characters; and in one great poem all is set before us.

This book seeks to map out the debt of Browning throughout his long poetic career to what Browning's Pope calls "the central truth." The truth of God and his place in Browning's experience has been a much-discussed subject. I desire to show the significance of the Incarnation in Browning's artistic unity. Thus I purpose to examine the major areas of Browning's interest in the monologues and lyrics: religion, art, and love. In dealing with any of these subjects in a poem, Browning's characteristic method is to solve the "problem" of the poem by some kind of incarnational experience.

The book is organized so that Browning's attempt to achieve the moment of spiritual unity through the Incarnation is examined first in the religious monologues. Then to this theme is added Browning's attempt to realize the moment of aesthetic unity in the art monologues. Both of these subjects, religion and art, have their minor roles in the third aspiration, for physical unity in the love poems. The culmination of Browning's genius is *The Ring and the Book*. Here the three themes of religion, art, and love reach their fruition; aspiration becomes achievement in the moment of composite unity. Thus many threads are interwoven as the book proceeds; they fit more and more closely together, until finally the total fabric has been unrolled. It is a mistake to look for the finished tapestry in the first dash of the shuttle. Only with *The Ring and the Book* does the whole complex pattern of Browning's use of the Incarnation become clear. A final chapter simply surveys the last years of Browning's activity to indicate that "the central truth" remains the informing principle.

A secondary theme in this book, related intimately to the first, is Browning's consideration of the concept of time. By means of the Incarnation, Browning came to understand that the philosophic problem of time, of history, of past and future, is solved by "the central truth." Furthermore, time concerns Browning in a special aesthetic way in his poetry. The moment of unity, the "moment one and infinite," as he calls it, is very difficult to express in the temporal sequence of line after line of poetry. Again it is the incarnational experience which unifies temporal existence, just as it does religion, aesthetics, and the science of love. Browning came to know the Incarnation as the supreme analogue for the poet's creative activity, as the unique means, examined in very different contexts, by which the unitive moment could be captured in a line of verse.

I have assumed the reality of the Incarnation, not as a remote theological proposition (a course of inquiry which has bedevilled Browning criticism for eighty years with numerous heresy-hunters), but as an historic truth alive in Browning's experience. The Incarnation is not a religious framework over which to drape the heavily curtained theology of Browning's poetry. The Incarnation affects Browning to the depths of his being as a man. It is in his poetry that we can discover the extent of its penetration into his experience. I have selected and arranged the poems arbitrarily to give a representative and structured approach to the subject. I do not for a moment suppose that Browning self-consciously sought to develop such a scheme as that presented in this book. I seek simply to elucidate the interrelationships of Browning's ideas, and to show how they are applied with an astonishing consistency and power in his writings.

The centrality of the Incarnation in Browning's religious thought has been noted by almost every commentator. In "Browning and Incarnation" (an M.A. thesis completed under the direction of Professor F. E. L. Priestley at the University of Toronto, and unfortunately unpublished), Miss Beryl Stone has shown the absolute centrality of the

Incarnation in Browning's life and poetry up to 1860. I owe much of my background in Browning's early thought as it developed in his poetry and the letters to Miss Stone's thesis.

It was in his graduate seminar at University College that Professor F. E. L. Priestley expounded the Trinitarian pattern in Browning, giving full place to the Incarnation, especially in his treatment of *A Death in the Desert*. Professor Priestley suggested that an examination of such patterns could be extended valuably throughout the Browning canon, and this book is the product of that extension. He has always been most illuminating, and, more valuable still in a good teacher, stimulating, so that if this book has any merit, the honour is his.

My thanks are also due to many other teachers, among whom I must mention the late Professors A. S. P. Woodhouse and H. S. Wilson, and Professor Northrop Frye. The Editors of the University of Toronto Press have made working with them a delightful and heartening activity. Many friends, and particularly two, have offered encouragement and constant hospitality, to make the writing of a book the pleasantest occupation. Finally, I gratefully thank my mother for many hours of painstaking care in the preparation of many manuscript drafts.

All quotations from Browning's poetry are from the Centenary Edition, *The Works of Robert Browning*, edited with introductions by F. G. Kenyon. All line references are to Kenyon's Centenary Edition; all other references in the text are page or section references.

This work has been published with the help of a grant from the Humanities Research Council, using funds provided by the Canada Council.

W. W.

Fredericton
Trinity Sunday, June 17, 1962

NOTE TO THE SECOND PRINTING

For this new printing I have taken the opportunity provided by the University of Toronto Press of making a number of minor typographical and factual corrections, and have added the Note on page 155.

Oxford, October 22, 1966　　　　　　　　　　　　　　　　W. W.

TO MY PARENTS

CONTENTS

THE CENTRAL TRUTH

TIME, THE INCARNATION,
AND THE POET

I knew, I felt, . . . what God is, what we are,
What life is. . . . (*Paracelsus,* V, 638)

What's time to us? (*Sordello,* V, 26)
. . . Fit to the finite his infinity. (*Sordello,* VI, 499)
. . . We circumscribe omnipotence. (*A Pillar at Sebzevar*)

BROWNING FACED the complex religious and scientific situation of his day by stressing the central importance of the Incarnation in the redemption of all time, and of man in time. The Incarnation provided an adequate explanation for what to Browning was the mystery of life. Duration of life in the time-process meant that the historically conscious poet had to come to terms with the meaning of history; for Browning, history is best interpreted in the light of the Incarnation.

The assaults on faith which presented themselves as very real problems to Browning came partially out of the nineteenth-century inheritance from eighteenth-century "rationalism," and partly from the tremendous advances in the natural, physical, and theoretical sciences. These two great streams of thought became fused and confused, the one leading chiefly to the Higher Criticism (with its at least nodding acknowledgment of debt to scientific method), and the other to the New Science (with its own debt to rationalism repaying the balance). These movements have led to a dichotomy which places religion on the one hand and science on the other, and calls the area between them a conflict. It was into this conflict that Browning threw himself against the Higher Critics of the Bible. He saw the tendency which was emerging from the attack, as it moved from valuable biblical research into unilateral assaults on faith in general. He responded with the subjective answer of the poet, put into the objective guise of speakers in a series of dramatic monologues.

Browning presents a highly individual interpretation of an orthodox theological position. There is a significant pattern of development not only in his writings, but also in his life: a progression from an initial state of naive belief into some form of "rational" agnosticism and indifference, and on through this to mature belief. Browning, whose well-to-do father in middle life had left the Church of England to become a dissenter and whose mother was a Congregationalist, had a strict evangelical upbringing. To the staunch piety of his mother Browning owed much of the foundation of his religious views. He came under the influence of Eliza and Sarah Flower in his youth, along with their guardian, the Reverend W. J. Fox, the prominent Unitarian of South Place Chapel. After Browning read Shelley and Voltaire, he toyed with atheism and vegetarianism for two years when he was about fourteen, and eventually became a deist. From these encounters he recovered the core of his evangelical piety, while Unitarianism, with its long tradition of free-thinking, left him open to scepticism. Thereafter it was a slow struggle to his position of 1850 when in *Christmas-Eve and Easter-Day* he presented the fruit of his labour, the acknowledgment of his debt to doubt in the acceptance of Christianity. Throughout the rest of his poetry Browning fought a constant battle with his belief, but it is important to realize that it was a belief that was tenaciously held and defended all the more strongly because of his own doubts about it.

The writings of Browning show an active searching for the answers to problems in his own life. In the poetry and prose we find a gradual movement towards adequate answers for his problems of faith, aesthetics, and love. In Browning there never seems to be a final position, since he always doubts, and then accepts, and then doubts again. Time after time we find Browning returning to the same problem in his poetry to examine another aspect of it. But from *Christmas-Eve and Easter-Day* onwards, he has reached a workable, inclusive, and Christian point of reference for his poetry.

Browning's method of proceeding to a religious belief by doubt and by an argument based on love in the human personality leads him to one primary belief: the mystery of the Incarnation of Jesus Christ. In an unpublished Master's dissertation, "Browning and Incarnation," Beryl Stone has demonstrated convincingly the central position given to Christ's Incarnation in Browning's religious thought *and poetry*:

The symbolic act of the Incarnation of Christ offered Browning an analogy of his own experience as a creative artist. The artist enjoys a vision of the truth which must be shared with humanity. As God clothed himself in human flesh, so the poet speaks in words the vision that he has seen. If the artist manages to convey in language the truth of his vision, he will have unfolded something of the Divine Word in his human words. He will share in the redeeming work of Christ as he liberates men from the tyranny of error and the bondage of self.[1]

Miss Stone has argued by using Browning's letters and poems that the Incarnation comes increasingly to the fore in his early poetry. It is very important to note that in the movement of Browning's thought through the years, that doctrine remains at the centre. But its position is constantly challenged, not least by the poet himself.

Browning answers the critics of Christianity by asserting the traditional faith of the Gospels, of the primitive Church, and of the Fathers. Because of this fact, the doctrine of the Incarnation is understood in relation to and is interpreted by a traditional past. That is, the Incarnation is placed, both in its factuality and in its interpretation, in the historical process. To poetry, the Incarnation is the central symbolic archetype operating in the Western tradition of literature, representing by analogy the artist's work in clothing his thoughts with words. So we are led to the connection between the Incarnation and tradition, history, and the time-process. Browning saw a valuable poetic and philosophic dependence of time upon the Incarnation, and although he does not elaborate a philosophy of time, he incorporates one into his poetry. Frequently the dependence of time upon the Incarnation is a controlling factor in the thought-structure of a poem. But to understand Browning's thought we need to have a vocabulary and framework in which to study it. We can do no better than to use the vocabulary and framework of the Bible where we find the same close association of time and the Incarnation of Christ.

In the Old Testament there is no way of distinguishing between realistic and chronological time, as represented in the New Testament by the terms *chronos* and *kairos*. *Kairos* refers to realistic time which is identified by its content, and must be accompanied by opportunity.

---

[1] "Browning and Incarnation," M.A. thesis, University of Toronto (1957), iii.

Man must respond to the opportunity provided by time with an appropriate action, as in "seed time and harvest." Man makes a response to God's activity in time, even in going to bed and rising from it. While the Old Testament authors wrote about *a* time of God's activity, the New Testament writer knows that he is writing about *the* time of God's action in history. In Christ *the* time, the *kairos*, has come—and the content of this time is the atoning life, death, and resurrection of the Son of God. Man is brought to his greatest opportunity, and of him is demanded his greatest response. The historical fact which confronts man is Jesus Christ, who comes at the appointed time (*kairos*), the time suitable for an undertaking, the fixed and determined day which has been so fixed by divine decision. The *kairos* of the present moment has to be redeemed, as St. Paul says, on the basis of the significant *kairoi* of the past—the birth, death, and resurrection of Christ.

Another New Testament term for time is *aion*, referring to the unlimited extension of time into eternity. Thus it stands for the time in God's plan when the eschatological drama will take place at the end of the ages. It is also the "coming age" which had appeared in Christ as the advent of the messianic kingdom. It is the NOW of salvation (the *yom Yahweh*) persisting throughout the Christian era, having its *foci* in the life of the individual and the life of the Church. Christ, in his revealing and redemptive work, is the bearer of God's lordship over the time, filling the *kairoi* with their content, ushering in the *aion* of God, making the whole a known redemptive process.

In the New Testament (Mark 1:15), Jesus is represented as saying, "The time (*kairos*) is fulfilled, and the Kingdom of God is at hand." The *kairos* cannot be understood merely as an especially significant time or a critical opportunity. Jesus comes into Galilee uttering a proclamation that gathers about his person all the hopes of Jewish expectation, all the aspirations for deliverance and restoration, all the yearnings for the Messiah. Christ focused all these hopes in himself, and connected them with *the* significant "time" in Israel's past when she was rescued from bondage in Egypt and constituted as God's nation. Israel was saved "at that day" at the Red Sea, and now a new kingdom, a new day, and a new "time" is inaugurated as the old dispensation is fulfilled. God is no longer content to be active in history, but becomes incarnate *in* history as the centre and end of it all.

The meaning of secular history is found in the revealed *kairoi*, but man is not to seek to know when the completion, the *parousia*, the *eskaton*, will come: "It is not for you to know the times (*chronoi*) or seasons (*kairoi*) which the Father hath set within his own authority" (Acts 1:7). Time, history, and eternity are most closely related in the "last time" of the *parousia*. But the "last time" has come, and the *parousia* will only reveal him who is and has all along been at the centre of the process. History is given an ultimate significance because succession is done away with, and is replaced by fulfilment.

Christ in history as the full, perfect, and complete revelation of God in love, makes all previous and subsequent events part of redemptive history. And all of the whole cosmic time-in-Christ is *the* moment in the eternity of God. It is this moment that so concerns Browning no less in his love poetry than in his religious poetry. In Christ, time has been divided anew, because the centre of time has been reached. However, the final apocalypse, or revelation, or fulfilment, is still to come. An intense hope for the future, so characteristic of Christianity (and closely related to Browning's optimism), is explained by the fact that the centre of time is not the object of hope in itself, for it is an already-occurred fact. The centre of time gives support to a future hope and expectation of an imminent end in the coming of the fulness of the Kingdom.

Towards this kind of philosophic and theological statement of the problem of time Browning moves in his poetic activity. The *kairos* of the exact time which had been ordained from the beginning is the moment in Browning when two lovers meet and in that moment can enjoy some of the suspension of temporal activity in the contemplation of eternity. That is the time between time and eternity when the temporal is transfixed by the eternal and life takes on new meaning because of the new vision which comes in the moment of apperception. The *kairos* has both occasion and content, both perhaps dimly perceived in the experience of the speaker in the poem, but the content forces a critical decision which must be made in the light of the occasion's experience. Browning regards the moment as a critical one which radically judges all of the experience before it, and contains the potential for great change after it. The moment then has to be used in the way that is most valuable, and for the poet that means in the light of the absolute value of love. Here again is the close connection that we detected earlier between the *kairos* and the Incarnation of the God of Love. We shall see how Browning links these ideas of time and the moment to the doctrine of the Incarnation.

When the Divine Word became flesh (John 1: 14), then were all of the prophecies of Israel fulfilled (Acts 10: 43), for the desire of all nations had come into time (Haggai 2: 7), and had changed it from being the successions of mutations into the acceptable year of the Lord of grace (Isaiah 61: 2). For primitive Christianity, salvation is a time process, and time is always connected with the redemptive process (Matthew 26: 18, Mark 1: 15). The "fulfilment" or "completion" of time (Ephesians 1: 10) points to the goal of the process, the *telos*, when the eschatological drama begins, and *the* time is at hand (Revelations 1: 3, 22: 10). What is significant for our purposes is that all of these elements are unified as the eternity of the present moment in the oneness of Christ.[2]

Although the explanation of the Incarnation as the Word of God becoming flesh in Jesus Christ is itself simple enough, there have been many theological controversies over a precise statement of the doctrine, and each controversy has ended with a dogmatic pronouncement of the triumphing orthodoxy. The doctrine of the Incarnation may be traced historically through the letters of St. Paul, the Gospels, the rest of the New Testament, and the writings of Ignatius of Antioch, Irenaeus, Tertullian, Athanasius, Hilary, Leo, and other early Fathers of both East and West. Conciliar definition was more important, although patristic thought lay at the roots of the early creeds. Nicaea (A.D. 325) gave rise to the creed that bears the city's name, and the creed was re-affirmed at Chalcedon in A.D. 451. But it was the Chalcedonian "Definition of Faith" which most characterized the council, and which put the New Testament teaching into the technical language of the professional theologian:

Therefore, following the holy Fathers, we all with one accord teach men to acknowledge one and the same Son, our Lord Jesus Christ, at once complete in Godhead and complete in manhood, truly God and truly man, consisting also of a reasonable [i.e., rational] soul and body; of one substance ($\delta\mu oo\acute{u}\sigma\iota o\varsigma$) with the Father as regards His Godhead, and at the same time of one substance with us as regards his manhood; like us in all respects, apart from sin; as regards his Godhead, begotten of the Father before the ages, but yet as regards his manhood begotten, for us men and for our salvation, of Mary the Virgin, the God-bearer ($\Theta EOT\acute{O}KO\Sigma$); one and the same Christ, Son, Lord, Only-begotten, recognized in two natures, without confusion, without change,

[2]Cullmann, *Christ and Time*, 32, and Marsh, *The Fulness of Time, passim.*

without division, without separation, the distinction of natures being in no way annulled by the union, but rather the characteristics of each nature being preserved and coming together to form one person and subsistence (ὑπόστασις) not as parted or separated into two persons, but one and the same Son and Only-begotten God the Word, Lord Jesus Christ; even as the prophets from earliest time spoke of him, and our Lord Jesus Christ himself taught us, and the creed of the Fathers has handed down to us.[3]

The formulations of Chalcedon continued to be interpreted by theologians and councils of both the East and the West in, for example, Anselm, Aquinas, Calvin, Luther, and Hooker, to take us up to A.D. 1600. All this learned scholastic debate was intended to clarify the essential truth of the Incarnation, that somehow God entered history in a radical way by robing his majesty in our human vesture by assuming humanity itself. It was that historic truth, known to Browning rather as a reality of his experience than as a Christological dogma, which so permeated his thinking. Much critical labour has been expended on Browning's religious opinions, and many irrelevant facts have been collected to "prove" his heresies. These trials of Browning's orthodoxy will not concern us here, because we shall concentrate on the important connection between the Incarnation itself (not how he viewed it or any theory or dogma about it) and the aesthetic process. Just how Browning deviates from the norm is not our concern, because that examination has already been made. We do not wish to judge Browning as a theologian; we do have to analyse and relate those places in his writing where theology plays an informing role.[4]

In Browning there seems to be little emphasis on the other primary Christological doctrine, the Atonement of Christ. Critics have repeatedly seen in Browning's neglect of the Atonement a defective view of sin and its cure. But to Browning, as well as to the rather stubborn Church which has refused to define the Atonement dogmatically, the Incarnation can be understood not only in terms of its nature, but also in terms of its purpose—to present the Second Adam to take away the sins of the world. Similarly, the doctrine of the Trinity does not receive major discussion in Browning apart from the analogues of it, which are recurrent themes. Mrs. Sutherland Orr, in her article "Religious Opinions of Robert Browning," suggests that there seems to be a duality in Browning's view of divinity. She argues that on the one hand he saw

[3]Bettenson, H. S., *Documents of the Christian Church* (Oxford University Press, 1953), 73; Council of Chalcedon, *Actio V, Mansi vii*, 116 f.   [4]See the Bibliographical note on p. 155

God as the infinite, omnipotent deity, the "Supreme Being of meta-physics," and on the other as the personal and loving God who shows joy and sorrow in the Person of Christ. But the duality which is suggested here is not borne out by the extensive use that Browning makes of the analogical principle applied to the Trinity through the three souls in man, and the tri-partite division of the aspects of the deity into Power, Knowledge, and Love. Browning's doctrine of poetic inspiration is essentially pentecostal in its nature; inspiration is also the means by which the lover and the beloved reach the moment of union and understanding. The view which sees Browning's theology as deficient because of a supposed dualism is superficial. The place of the Holy Spirit in his thought is not explicitly expounded in his poetry, but it is everywhere present.

It is of the utmost importance to stress the fact that Browning is not a professional theologian. He sees the world as the Christian poet sees it, that is, by means of an aesthetic as well as a spiritual experience. But because of the all-inclusiveness of the Christian concept of the Incarnation, the poet and time are viewed as related to the Christ-event, and take their meaning from that event. By exploring the aesthetic process as it is related to Christian thought, the poet may come to terms with himself, others, the world, and God, as Browning has done. The Incarnation, then, can be seen as a central unifying concept in Browning; by examining his views on the Incarnation and its role in the redemption of the time process, we should better see the poetic method and significant structure of his writing.

Time, the Incarnation, and the poetic experience become ordered in the aesthetic pattern of a poem so that the poet's own personal emotions are ordered. Faith and doubt are to some extent rationalized, but they themselves are expressed in poetry, the giving of significant and ordered and artistic written form to thought. They lead to an awareness and acceptance of the situation and the moment, the place and the time of the poetic experience, and in the Incarnation is realized the ultimate value of each. We seem to have come full circle back to the point of beginning: only the Incarnation can give full meaning to life. For the Christian poet the Incarnation is the symbol incarnate of which all other symbols in literature are but imitations. It is by analogy with this act of God that the poet may attempt to create—to give flesh to his words as God did to the Word. For Browning this becomes a tremendous problem of communication—the putting of his thoughts into words. It is further complicated by the fact that poetry is a social art, depending on some communication of ideas just as Christianity must also communicate the Word by words. Furthermore, Browning wished to overcome the linear restrictions of verse in the rendering of simultaneous events or emotions. To do this he naturally was concerned with the problem of time in an extraordinary way. It was by means of the Incarnation with its almost archetypal symbol of eternity in time's moment that some sort of a solution could be achieved.

Now the thought must be made word in creative activity, and then, as an additional step in the process, it must be made flesh in the actor or the *persona*. Here too the limitations of language over time present a formidable problem. Again the solution lies in the Incarnation:

> I say, the acknowledgment of God in Christ
> Accepted by thy reason, solves for thee
> All questions in the earth and out of it,
> And has so far advanced thee to be wise.
>
> *A Death in the Desert*, 474–7

II

SPIRITUAL UNITY:
POETRY AND RELIGION

This one earth, out of all the multitude
Of peopled worlds, as stars are now supposed,—
Was chosen, and no sun-star of the swarm,
For stage and scene of Thy transcendent act. . . .

(*The Ring and the Book*, The Pope, X, 1336–9)

1. BACKGROUND: THE EARLY POETRY TO 1850

William Temple, in an early essay on Browning read at Balliol in 1904, asserts that for Browning the "climax of history, the crown of philosophy, and the consummation of poetry is unquestionably the Incarnation."[1] Temple argues that the doctrine inspires and informs the poetry from *Saul* on through *Karshish*, *A Death in the Desert*, and *Christmas-Eve and Easter-Day*. The position which Browning slowly came to in the early poetry is really the inspiration and informative concept in the later poetry too, so that, as Temple concludes, the Incarnation "is no solitary truth struggling for supremacy with other truths—it is itself the sum total of all truths, and if once realized will take the place of experience, of thought, nay of worship itself." That kind of experience of the Incarnation leads to a religious individualism in Browning which is limited in two important directions. The corporate action and life of the whole body of believers in the Incarnation is forgotten, and along with it goes the expression of corporate life in the sharing of common sacramental action and life. Browning's background was fostered in this rejection of Church and sacraments by his

[1] *Religious Experience and Other Essays*, 51–2.

inheritance of an independent Congregationalism from his mother and Unitarianism from the Flowers, and their guardian, W. J. Fox. Shelley and Voltaire provided other early influences, leading to the Messiah-type of Shelleyan hero in *Pauline*. Love is significant in the poem, but it is incomplete; there is a desire for the revelation of God, and the longing for a loving God, but there is no means of coming to know such a God. In *Sordello* and *Paracelsus* Browning becomes aware of the inadequacy of a Unitarian Christology which makes Christ simply an ethical examplar. He slowly came to realize that the human soul could not rise of its own to grasp the fire of heavenly love; love somehow must be brought to earth as a gift.

In *Paracelsus*, as W. O. Raymond has pointed out,[2] Browning stated the themes which were to be the leading and controlling ideas of his poetry. Raymond's argument is at complete variance with the unsubstantiated view expressed by Stopford Brooke: "When *Paracelsus* was published in 1835 Browning had fully thought out, and in that poem fully expressed, his theory of God's relation to man, and of man's relation to the universe around him, to his fellow men, and to the world beyond." On the contrary, Browning was to develop all his life, but it is a development which follows the patterns either explicitly stated or else implied in the lines of *Paracelsus*. Browning's addition to Aprile's dying speech in Part II shows Aprile as a kind of love incarnate, and also indicates the early interest of Browning in the Incarnation:

> Man's weakness is his glory—for the strength
> Which raises him to heaven and near God's self
> Came spite of it. God's strength his glory is,
> For thence came with our weakness sympathy,
> Which brought God down to earth, a man like us!

Browning was to explore the vocation of the poet in terms of the Incarnation, for, as I have said, the work of the poet in clothing his ideas in words is analogous to the mystery of the Incarnation as God clothed his Word in flesh. The vocation to be a poet concerned Browning deeply, as we learn from Edmund Gosse, who records how the aged Browning talked with him about his own early vocation: "He sat and talked of his own early life and aspirations; how he marvelled, as he looked back, at the audacious obstinacy which had made him, when a

[2] *The Infinite Moment*, 156.

youth, determine to be a poet and nothing but a poet."[3] One is immediately reminded of Milton's Sonnet VII, "How soon hath Time," as having the same sort of literary, religious, and emotional genesis. The poet's vocation (which Browning was working out in these early poems) was next considered in the relation of the artist to his medium in *Sordello*, where Browning uses Sordello as the analogy of Christ—as a Christ-type in a given situation. Browning told his friend Furnivall[4] that the central theme of the poem is contained in the following lines:

> . . . —to display completely here
> The mastery another life should learn,
> Thrusting in time eternity's concern.

> (I, 564–6)

Sordello, for all his success in the kingdom of song, is unable to clothe his perceptions in language. He cannot thrust into time the concern of eternity as happened at the Incarnation. It is exactly the meeting of time and eternity with the fact of the Incarnation that is of supreme significance to the poet. In the temporality of the line of poetry, even in the special restrictions of the written line, it is impossible for Sordello to capture that sort of contemporaneity and simultaneity of event and thought which allows eternity to bloom in the moment of time. Sordello, after all, is described as "this incarnation of the People's hope" (IV, 381), and yet, although he has explored all of the means of poetic expression and the different kinds of poet, he cannot "fit to the finite his infinity" (VI, 499). The failure of Sordello, unlike that of Paracelsus, has been a failure in love. In the three poems, *Pauline*, *Paracelsus*, and *Sordello* the hero is struggling with the dual problem of communicated revelation and vocation. This is analogous to the activity of God. If the revelation is really to be communicated, and if it is effectively communicating so that a sense of vocation is aroused, then love and self-sacrifice must be involved in the activity to an extraordinary degree. That is the spiritual dimension which each hero sees from a distance, but cannot experience. The poet, however, in the intense vision of his creative activity, moves across the limiting distance into the experience of love and self-sacrifice. Here his action is analo-

[3]*Robert Browning Personalia*, 84.
[4]Duffin, *Amphibian*, 231.

gous to Christ's redemptive work. Sordello concluded that his task as
poet is to live the life of significant toil:

> Here is the Crowd, whom I with freest heart
> Offer to serve, contented for my part
> To give life up in service,—only grant
> That I do serve. . . .
>
> (VI, 387–90)

It was Christ who came among men as the Suffering Servant, among us
as "one who serves." But Sordello spurned some such step eventually,
and so failed to act in loving self-sacrifice.

Pippa, as the child of God and the child of Nature, allows Browning
to explore in her the results of the manifestation of humility, love, and
joy. Then, in 1850, *Christmas-Eve and Easter-Day* marks the turning-
point in Browning's thought as he fled the deserts of Shelleyan deism
along the path that had already been clearly indicated in the movement
through *Pauline*, *Paracelsus*, *Sordello*, and *Pippa Passes*. He had been
influenced by the death of his mother and by the religious convictions of
Elizabeth Barrett. *Christmas-Eve and Easter-Day* was published after
Browning had released the fragment of *Saul* to the press, but before he
had worked out all of the implications, permitting him to bring the work
to completion only after he had solved the problems presented in
Christmas-Eve and Easter-Day. In *Christmas-Eve* Browning shows an
awareness of the consummation of time in the Incarnate Lord of Time:

> Earth breaks up, time drops away,
> In flows heaven, with its new day
> Of endless life, when He who trod,
> Very man and very God. . . .
>
> (X, 583–6)

All of the concerns of external religious worship are rejected as Browning can make his personal choice for Christ in the present time. He
has had his series of visions, and has meditated upon them; they have
brought him to the place where he must accept or reject the truth that
the visions have kept veiled from him. The moment of critical choice,
of which we shall see so much later, is faced squarely, and Browning
answers with clarity and certainty, "I choose here!"

Browning could not complete his *Saul* until he had worked out his

Christology in *Christmas-Eve and Easter-Day*.[5] *Saul* remains the tangible testimony to Browning's faith in the Incarnation, and the two versions show clearly the path that he found to faith. The path to faith was also the path to a more carefully formulated poetic theory. Browning had said in *Sordello* that there are three kinds of poet, one purely descriptive, one who tells the quiddity of what he sees, and the highest kind, who gives the gift of seeing to his readers:

> So occupied, then, are we: hitherto,
> At present, and a weary while to come,
> The office of ourselves,—nor blind nor dumb,
> And seeing somewhat of man's state,—has been,
> For the worst of us, to say they so have seen;
> For the better, what it was they saw; the best
> Impart the gift of seeing to the rest. . . .
>
> (III, 862–8)

In the first two lines, Browning connects what he is going to say about the function of the poet with a concept of time as past, present, and future. The visionary poet who will give seeing to the rest sees into the store of the future, and so his function is prophetic. In the *Essay on Shelley* Browning's poetic convictions emerge more explicitly, giving us the doctrine of the objective and the subjective poet, with "the whole poet's function of beholding with an understanding keenness the universe, nature and man, in their actual state of perfection in imperfection." In the poet, "one earnest and unextorted assertion of belief should outweigh, as a matter of testimony, many assertions of unbelief." Thus the poet who has had the vision of religious truth, and who presents it freely in an "assertion of belief," and does it with such artistry that he gives to others the gift of seeing that vision—*that* poet is the best kind of poet. So Browning can conclude with his stress on

[5]Miss Stone writes about the influences on Browning at this time (in "Browning and Incarnation," 97–8): "Browning in 1845 published *Saul*, aware of its potentialities for the future exploration and demonstration of his poetic theory. In 1851 the effect of Milsand's article [*Revue des Deux Mondes*, 15 August 1851] assisted him greatly in the clear formulation of that theory in the *Essay on Shelley*. In the years between 1851 and 1855, when the completed poem appeared, he distinctly recognized Christ as the 'Son of David' and completed the poem on the note of vision. I do not mean that Browning did not know in 1845 that Christ was of the 'house and lineage of David'; rather I suggest that the events of the interval—his marriage and the warmth and light which his love for Elizabeth Barrett brought, the thoughts to which the death of his mother and the birth of his son in 1849 brought him, the formulation of his poetic credo in 1851, the period of quiet retirement which marked the first years in Italy—all these events provided background and impetus for deepening insight."

the ultimate nature of God as being, omnipotence, love, expressing himself in terms of beauty and goodness; and all of these are made relevant to man's situation by the Incarnation as the expression of God's omnipotence in love:

In the hierarchy of created minds, it is the presence of the highest faculty that gives first rank, in virtue of its kind, not degree; . . . this I call his [Shelley's, or the ideal poet's] simultaneous perception of Power and Love in the absolute, and of Beauty and Good in the concrete, while he throws, from his poet's station between both, swifter, subtler, and more numerous films for the connection of each, than have been thrown.

Browning was beginning to see how the Incarnation closely linked God's action with the poet's function of discerning and clothing in language the "pure white light."

The religious conclusions to which Browning came after the completion of his three monologues, *Christmas-Eve, Easter-Day*, and *Saul*, and the poetic theory which he had progressively formulated through *Pauline, Paracelsus, Sordello*, and the *Essay on Shelley*, were brought together intellectually by Browning's meditation on the Incarnation. Browning's religious and aesthetic positions were unified, but there still remained a number of problems to solve. The rest of his life was occupied in the careful exploration of the avenues of affirmation and doubt; his poetry chronicles that exploration.

Browning was faced with the problem of time in *Pauline, Paracelsus*, and *Sordello*, it is true, but in these poems he was concerned with the poet's expression of the simultaneous occurrence of events or thoughts in the restrictions of the linear line of verse which itself requires the passage of time to be read and understood. When Browning had fortified his religious position after *Christmas-Eve and Easter-Day*, he could consider a different kind of simultaneity in *Saul* so that David in his supreme moment of vision could cry, "See the Christ stand!" The moment of vision is also the moment of Incarnation. It is fitting "to the finite his infinity"; it is the eternal present which is seen wholly, and comprehended with unusual clarity. This moment is a constant aesthetic problem for the artist, and Browning's solution is to solve the aesthetic by means of the religious. He can see the eternal moment in time which is also the moment that gives significance to the whole poem. There is no doubt that the climax of *Saul* is that great epiphany, because then the suffering of Saul himself is given its relative value. Now Browning has to apply what he has learned in the unification of the aesthetic and the religious processes to other themes.

Christmas-Eve prepared for Browning's future development of religious themes, and in *Easter-Day*, as W. C. DeVane says, he "built his conception of a modern Christian, discussing this time not man's relation to the various creeds [as in *Christmas-Eve*], but his direct relation to Christ, who lived and died on earth for him and rose from the dead on Easter-Day."[6] By means of doubt Browning is discovering "How very hard it is to be a Christian!" He is hunting for grounds of belief in which there must be a place for art, since art is a foreshadowing of heaven; there must be a place for intellect, even though it is earth-bound and restricted epistemologically to the senses; and nature also must be included in the grounds of belief. Each of these is rejected as incomplete in itself. Browning shows that nature, intellect, and art, his constant concerns from the writing of *Pauline*, amply demonstrate the power and wisdom of God, the attributes of omnipotence and omniscience, but they do not have a place for the one quality in man which Browning finds to be unlimited—love. Many of Browning's favourite themes are gathered into this poem: the necessity of doubt is stressed in its role as the bulwark of faith; nature shows the power and wisdom of God in all of its beauty; art "supplants, gives mainly worth to nature" (xxv) as the earnest of heaven; and mind, though limited by the senses, still strives to make "the finite comprehend infinity" (xxviii). All these areas of experience are found to be inadequate means of approaching the mystery of the Incarnation without the affirmation that "Love is best" (xxx). Here is one of the central statements of Browning's poetic and religious creed. The love shown in the Incarnation as the supreme revelation of the nature of God not only motivates the religious monologues, but links them with the monologues on the subjects of painting, music, and romantic love. By means of the theology which Browning has developed he is able to view painting, music, and love as the media in which he tries to fit the infinite to the finite, to produce the timeless, to express through art the whole meaning of love in a philosophy of life within the finite limitations of the poetic line. These three areas of Browning's poetic achievement, religion, art, and love, will be examined as we consider the most important poems from 1850 to the *Dramatis Personae* of 1864.

[6] *A Browning Handbook*, 202.

2. THE RELIGIOUS MONOLOGUES

An Epistle (1855 in *Men and Women*) grew, according to W. C. DeVane, out of Browning's meditation upon and study for *Christmas-Eve and Easter-Day*, and, indeed, it shows the central concern that Browning felt for the Incarnation, and the place that an honest but unprejudiced doubt would play in its apprehension. Browning is now dealing with a known historical period. He regarded the birth of Christ as the first great crisis that the world had to face. In the person of Karshish, the Arab physician, the reader is invited to face that crisis as he did. Karshish tries very hard to view the miracle of Lazarus as a medical problem from the standpoint of an open-minded physician, but again and again he returns to the controlling concept of the poem:

> The very God! think, Abib; dost thou think?
> So, the All-Great, were the All-Loving too—
>
> (304-5)

Karshish is using the letter to clarify his own mind. The actual exercise of writing, of ordering his own thoughts on the case, serves to consolidate his position. The artistic experience is the means of ordering the life-situation. Here is the same process that was at work in Browning's own situation when he wrote *Christmas-Eve and Easter-Day*, and it is likely that we have it again in *An Epistle* itself. From such parallel situations, some of the poem's many ironies emerge.

The real centre of the poem is Christ. Karshish tells Abib that the "learned leech" perished in a tumult accused, ironically, of wizardry. Now, for the first time, Lazarus is said to be mad, a complete reversal of the earlier position of Karshish. The reason for the change is that the doctrine which he holds about Christ is blasphemous to Karshish, so it is rejected immediately, and yet... "it is strange," so he must examine it. He cannot put it from him, for

> This man so cured regards the curer, then,
> As—God forgive me! who but God himself,
> Creator and sustainer of the world,
> That came and dwelt in flesh on it awhile!
>
> (267-70)

Once more we shift back to the commonplace, with Karshish ironically apologizing for writing about such trivial matters as Christ and Lazarus, but again he returns to that symbolic landscape where the confrontation of the two faiths in Lazarus and Karshish took place, with its spotted moon, the ridge of broken hills, the wind behind him. One of the faiths is unshaken by the wind of doubt, the other is enveloped in it. The conclusion of the poem reminds one of the final vision of *Saul*:

> O Saul, it shall be,
> A Face like my face that receives thee; A Man like to me,
> Thou shalt love and be loved by, for ever: a Hand like this hand
> Shall throw open the gates of new life to thee! See the Christ stand!
>
> (XVIII, 309–12)

So Karshish comes back to the creation of each individual man that he had alluded to at the beginning, but now he is questioning and seeking a resolution of his doubt, a resolution based on love:

> So, through the thunder comes a human voice
> Saying, "O heart I made, a heart beats here!
> "Face, my hands fashioned, see it in myself!
> "Thou hast no power nor mayest conceive of mine,
> "But love I gave thee, with myself to love,
> "And thou must love me who have died for thee!"
>
> (306–11)

The parallels with *Saul* are apparent. Lazarus believed that Christ was God, and this leads to the dramatic ending when Karshish finds the blasphemous idea monstrous, but intensely compelling and attractive. He returns to it again and again, perhaps even indulging in conscious irony himself in the passage about the "ambitious Syrian," but Karshish is reaching forward, like David in *Saul* to the idea of a loving God who expresses his love in giving himself in human form. David's vision had the surety of prophecy; Lazarus' faith has the surety of knowledge; Karshish's knowledge has the required doubt that leads to faith.

Karshish has reached the critical moment in his life when he must act. He has the doubt that Browning believes is necessary for the health of the soul, and so he is prepared for the choice of will which is required for action. The Incarnation has led to the critical moment of choice. From this point on, all of Karshish's life will be lived in the light of this experience, the moment, for him, made eternity. As in *Easter-Day* the nature of God as Creator (that is, omnipotent) and as Sustainer (that is, interested, and knowing, or omniscient) is unquestioned ultimately.

Karshish has long since reached that position in his own faith. He has stumbled over the love of God, and finds the idea shattering. Browning has not finished with his treatment of the theme.

It was natural enough that Browning should have considered the impact of the Christian faith upon the heathen world after he had clarified his own religious position in *Christmas-Eve and Easter-Day* and *Saul*. He treated the scientific attitude of the Arab physician in *An Epistle*, and then turned to the cultured civilization of Greece in examining the attitude of the philosophic Greek, Cleon. *Cleon* was occasioned by Arnold's *Empedocles on Etna* (1852), a poem which Arnold did not reprint in the edition of 1853 that carried the famous preface which gave Arnold's ideas on poetry as well as his reasons for not reprinting *Empedocles*. *Empedocles* is a poem in which "suffering finds no vent in action," and when such situations occur, "they are painful, not tragic," and so Arnold did not republish the poem. Arnold urged poets to forsake timeliness in poetry for the greater and more classic virtues of choosing a significant subject, and striving for a unified total effect. It was Empedocles' fate to have missed the unity and wholeness which could have given his life its significance. He ultimately cannot follow his own doctrine of accepting the limitations which life imposes upon reason, and here there is a contrast with the life of imagination as seen in Callicles. Browning must have seen the parallels with his own examination of a similar theme in *Paracelsus*, and the omission of *Empedocles* from the edition of 1853, together with the poetic manifesto, must have set him thinking. Browning would see in Empedocles that type of the grotesque that always appealed to him, and yet he must have had sympathy for Arnold's plea for action, a doctrine close to Browning's heart also. DeVane writes: "Browning thought of Empedocles' condition as illustrating the logical result of Greek paganism, and created Cleon as a later philosopher and poet who represented the final product of Greek culture and who in the blindness of his pride rejected the Christianity which fulfilled every one of the needs already recognized by his own superb mind."[7] Browning sets up in *Cleon* the same pattern of attraction and repulsion as in *An Epistle*. Cleon writes of the Incarnation to Protus:

> Long since, I imaged, wrote the fiction out,
> That he or other God descended here

[7] *Ibid.*, 264.

And, once for all, showed simultaneously
What, in its nature, never can be shown,
Piecemeal or in succession;—showed, I say,
The worth both absolute and relative
Of all his children from the birth of time,
His instruments for all appointed work.

(115–22)

Cleon has, like Karshish, approached the Christian doctrine of love, but his intellectual pride will not allow him to go further, for "Their doctrine could be held by no sane man." Browning is offering to Arnold the Christian faith in a God of love to replace the suffering of Empedocles, and individual immortality to replace his despairing suicide.

Cleon is a valuable comment on Browning's attitude to Hellenism. Greek philosophy saw eternity as an escape from the exigencies of time into a timeless void. Greek art could offer no personal immortality more than the shadowy life in Hades of Greek religion. Greek sculpture was for Browning the typical example of classic anonymity. Protus' desire for fame is as fleeting, transient, and ephemeral as the garlands which Fame bestows. In the period of the first great crisis of the world, Browning presents Cleon as searching for individual immortality with its victory over time (which the Christian faith offered) but it is a judgment against Hellenism that it could not accept the Incarnation. Browning's opinion did not change, for in the *Parleying with Gerard De Lairesse* he has this to say:

Let things be—not seem,
I counsel rather,—do, and nowise dream!
Earth's young significance is all to learn:
The dead Greek lore lies buried in the urn
Where who seeks fire finds ashes. Ghost, foresooth!
What was the best Greece babbled of as truth?
"A shade, a wretched nothing,—sad, thin, drear,
Cold, dark, it holds on to the lost loves here, . . ."
                              Sad school
Was Hades!

(XIV, 389–405)

Only when classic art achieved its reflorescence in the Renaissance by the influence of Christianity was a true personal individuality able to emerge. For Browning the Renaissance is the second great period of crisis, and he treats that crisis in his Renaissance monologues. Hellenism failed partly because of its lack of realism, so that there could not be proper emphasis given to the creative work of the individual artist stamped with the personality of his own genius. Cleon had the genius and the artistry, but he shared the Hellenic failure in respect to realism. The crisis of civilization is the moment of critical choice, a choice illuminated by the Incarnation, which judges the choice. Karshish at least had doubts about the validity of his own faith; Cleon rejected the new faith totally. The crisis judged both men, and both men stand in Browning for whole civilizations. Greek philosophy had little appeal for him, while the East was a constant attraction. By means of the doubt which came at the critical moment, Karshish has already taken the first steps towards the acceptance of the Incarnation, and so time for him is being redeemed. Cleon exists in the cyclical world of mutation and cannot escape because he has rejected the avenue of doubt. Time for him is unredeemed. Cleon is a poet, a philosopher, and a king in his art, but the proper visionary function of each of these offices, to "impart the gift of seeing to the rest" (essentially an act of self-sacrifice) is distorted. The prophetic function of the poet is forfeited for philosophy. Karshish, as the most common of men, provides a complete contrast. He is tested in time by the Incarnation, and in every place where Cleon fails, he attains. He is not the poet, or prophet, or king, but by means of honest doubt he glimpses the vision, and actually exercises the proper poetic function of imparting the gift of the vision to Abib. That is how Browning sees his own function as poet. In the early poetry we have noted three significant sets of themes which we are now able to relate. *Pauline* ended with the vision of the Shelleyan hero seen in terms of the Sun-treader as poet-priest, prophet, and king in his art. *Paracelsus*, while still retaining the interest in the poet-priest concept, is more interested in the three "faculties," love, knowledge, and power. *Sordello* moves on again to incorporate both of these ideas from *Pauline* and from *Paracelsus* into a poetic theory of the different kinds of poet. We can see a movement from the Shelleyan functional characteristics of *Pauline* through the psychological abstractions of *Paracelsus* to the poetic theory of *Sordello*. Then in *Christmas-Eve and Easter-Day* these already-connected thoughts find their true centre in Browning's religious faith in the Incarnation. All of the concepts from the earlier poems are incorporated into the religious frame of reference, and these themes converge most significantly in the doctrine of the three souls in *A Death in the Desert*. It will help us to relate the ideas of these earlier poems with the controlling religious and aesthetic themes if we see the relevant passages set out:

> ... And I shall live
> With poets, calmer, purer still each time,
> And beauteous shapes will come for me to seize,
> And unknown secrets will be trusted me
> Which were denied the waverer once; but now
> I shall be priest and prophet as of old.
>
> *Pauline* (1014–19)

> ... some one creature yet to make,
> Some point where all those scattered rays should meet
> Convergent in the faculties of man.
> Power—neither put forth blindly, nor controlled
> Calmly by perfect knowledge; to be used
> At risk, inspired or checked by hope and fear:
> Knowledge—not intuition, but the slow
> Uncertain fruit of an enhancing toil,
> Strengthened by love: love—not serenely pure,
> But strong from weakness, like a chance-sown plant ...
> Love which endures and doubts and is oppressed
> And cherished, suffering much and much sustained,
> And blind, oft-failing, yet believing love,
> A half-enlightened, often-checkered trust. ...
>
> *Paracelsus* (V, 690–705)

> So occupied, then, are we: hitherto,
> At present, and a weary while to come,
> The office of ourselves,—nor blind nor dumb,
> And seeing somewhat of man's state,—has been,
> For the worst of us, to say they so have seen;
> For the better, what it was they saw; the best
> Impart the gift of seeing to the rest. ...
>
> *Sordello* (III, 826–32)

> Let
> What masters life disclose itself! Forget
> Vain ordinances, I have one appeal—
> I feel, am what I feel, know what I feel;
> So much is truth to me. What Is, then?
>
> *Sordello* (VI, 437–41)

In the hierarchy of creative minds, it is the presence of the highest faculty that gives first rank, in virtue of its kind, not degree. . . . This I call his simultaneous perception of Power and Love in the absolute, and of Beauty and Good in the concrete, while he throws from his poet's station between both, swifter, subtler, and more numerous films for the connection of each with each, than have been thrown. . . .

An Essay on Shelley

> . . . Three souls which make up one soul: first, to wit,
> A soul of each and all the bodily parts,
> Seated therein, which works, and is what Does,
> And has the use of earth, and ends the man
> Downward: but, tending upward for advice,
> Grows into, and again is grown into
> By the next soul, which, seated in the brain,
> Useth the first with its collected use,
> And feeleth, thinketh, willeth,—is what Knows:
> Which, duly tending upward in its turn,
> Grows into, and again is grown into
> By the last soul, that uses both the first,
> Subsisting whether they assist or no,
> And, constituting man's self, is what Is . . .
> What Does, what Knows, what Is; three souls, one man.

A Death in the Desert (84–103)

The functional categories of *Pauline* (poet-priest, prophet, and king), are applied as psychological abstractions in *Paracelsus* (love, knowledge, and power). The vision of Paracelsus is for a future "creature yet to make" who will combine these faculties in the person of man. *Sordello* applies the categories and the abstractions to the task of the poet in specifically metaphysical terms. In the *Essay on Shelley* Browning clearly speaks about the connection between the creative mind of the poet and his ability to communicate the absolutes and the concretes (Power, Love, and Beauty, Good). Finally, it is in *A Death in the Desert* that the religious, psychological, and aesthetic threads are drawn together in a comprehensive statement. The key-ideas of these passages could be set out in a table as follows:

Functional categories (*Pauline*)	Psychological abstractions (*Paracelsus*)	Poetic and aesthetic theory (*Sordello*)	Ontology (*A Death . . .*)
poet-priest	love	Makers-see	"what Is"
prophet	knowledge	poet of quiddity	"what Knows"
king	power	descriptive poet	"what Does"

We shall see later how these key ideas are elaborated in Browning's thought as the pattern is developed in his poetry.

Because the aesthetic theory of *Sordello* is connected to the psychological and religious thought of Browning, the Incarnation, as his central religious doctrine, has come to be regarded by him in psychological and aesthetic terms. The surface expression of the whole complex of thought is often on the simple functional category level of *Pauline*, but, as *A Death in the Desert* makes clear, the implications and direction of Browning's thought is now on the ontological level, while still including the psychological and aesthetic aspects. The connection in thought between *Cleon* and *An Epistle* may be demonstrated by relating the two poems to the pivotal work in Browning's thought, *Christmas-Eve and Easter-Day*. In each of these poems the central figure or speaker is characterized under the three catagories of poet, prophet, and king, and, from that comparison, a distinct pattern emerges which shows how Browning rejected the Greek, Cleon, because of his intellectual pride and accepted the Arab, Karshish, with his honest doubt. In *Christmas-Eve* the speaker (Browning himself, though dimly veiled) makes the decisive choice for Christ in the vision of eternity which comes when Browning is confronted with the crisis of history.

The customary biblical categories for viewing Christ are Priest, Prophet, and King. To move from the Jewish Christ to the Greek West to Cleon means that the categories become intellectualized. Browning's Cleon is a poet instead of a priest, a philosopher instead of a prophet, and a "king" in his art, instead of a king in deed. On the other hand, we move further to the East to the Arab Karshish, and find him to be neither poet nor priest, but physician; neither philosopher nor prophet, but believer and doubter; and not a king but a common man. By means of honest doubt Karshish is able to encounter faith and glimpse the vision that Cleon, for all his intellectual attainments, cannot reach. In communicating the vision to Abib, he fulfils the poet's essential task, for he has become what Sordello calls a "Maker-see." Both the Greek and the Arab civilizations are implicitly judged by the crisis of the Incarnation. Choice has to be made for or against Christ, as Browning was faced with the critical moment in *Christmas-Eve*. Karshish questions, just as Browning does. Cleon rejects his encounter, and so Browning rejects him and his philosophy. We should notice some other parallels also. Cleon comes to his encounter with the objective truth of Christ through the report of St. Paul; Karshish comes to his moment through the encounter with Lazarus. Browning comes to his encounter through Elizabeth Barrett, and by means of his own meditation as chronicled in *Christmas-Eve and Easter-Day.* The choice affirmed at the end of *Christmas-Eve,* "I choose here!", allows Browning to proceed to fulfil his vocation as a poet and prophet, thereby becoming a king in his art.

The pattern gives an indication of what we can expect in the rest of Browning's poetry. The speaker of a monologue is related to the poetic and religious centrality of Christ who illuminates every other position, showing it as perversion, denial, or affirmation. The illumination is especially clear in the various roles of poet-priest, prophet, and king that we have seen as constants in Browning from *Pauline,* and always they are touchstones for his own development as a poet.

Browning began his work on *Saul,* according to DeVane's chronology,[8] in January 1845, when he was reading Christopher Smart's *Song to David* and went on to read the rest of Smart's work. But he decided to publish it only as a fragment (the first nine sections), being unable to complete the movement of the poem until he had developed and consolidated his own religious position with the writing of *Christmas-Eve and Easter-Day* (1850). He could move from the ninth section to the conclusion only when his own experience of Christianity allowed, and the actual writing of the rest of the poem served to set in order his own experience, regulate it, and prepare it for future use. It has been demonstrated that Browning used Sir Thomas Wyatt's *Seven Penitential Psalms* for the framework of the completed *Saul,* following Wyatt closely throughout.[9] DeVane comments that because we know something of the genesis of *Saul,* it "serves as a means of measuring the development of Browning's religious ideas as well as a means of measuring his theory of poetry." It is clear that Browning saw David playing his harp as the type of the lyric poet. Even in the fragment David sings of the fatherhood of God and the brotherhood of man, and then of the joys of the senses in nature and earthly fame. All of these approaches are unable to move Saul, depicted as a Christ-type who is suffering in a cruciform position. But Saul's suffering is not voluntary, and is of an unknown cause. Saul is deep in what Carlyle calls the Centre of Indifference. The beginning of section x marks a

[8]*Ibid.,* 254, 255.
[9]McPeek, "The Shaping of Saul," in DeVane, *Handbook,* 257.

new outlook ("And lo, with that leap of my spirit,—heart, hand, harp and voice . . .") as David's poetic vision of the imagination develops ("Then fancies grew rife . . ."). The character of David in the poem is of vital importance. David as poet glimpses something of the revelatory vision, but his character is changed to that of the divinely inspired *vates*—the poet-prophet, as in the short one-line section xvi, one of the poem's chief points of balance:

> Then the truth came upon me. No harp more—no song more! outbroke—

In the completed poem, and the full vision, the poet exercised the prophetic faculty of the seer of the pagan world (a faculty denied to Cleon, significantly, who is the philosopher-poet whose visionary powers are limited by intellectual pride). David is now speaking *in propria persona* as the inheritor of the prophetic mantle of Judaism, and now he has moved to take over Saul's position as the Christ-type. He it is who is to be the King of Israel replacing Saul; he has had the vision and has known its poetic splendour as well as its religious truth. David is seeing the Christ as an extraordinary kind of "Love"-poet, as the Prophet and as King. In all of these roles David is the Old Testament type, as well as ancestor of Christ's manhood. In *Saul* the linking of the religious, the poetic, and the prophetic (in David as the Christ-type who himself sees the truth of the Incarnation) is vital to a consideration of Browning's religious philosophy and artistic theory. Browning thought of himself as a prophetic poet-king (and we should remember Shelley's famous doctrine that poets are the unacknowledged legislators of the world). Browning sees David as the same type, and it is not unlikely that there is some self-identification in the characterization. Browning's own position before *Christmas-Eve and Easter-Day* was not unlike that of the paralysed Saul of the first version of the poem. Then when Browning had worked out his religious views in the poem of 1850, he could see himself in a newer and more intense light. The way out of Saul's suffering was through the vision of David which Browning made his own. The high place which Browning accordingly gives to the poet is attested by his letter to Ruskin of December 10, 1855, in which he says that "a poet's affair is with God, to whom he is accountable, and of whom is his reward. . . ."[10] The three roles of prophet, poet, and king are useful for Browning as categories about which to

---

[10]Collingwood, *Life and Work of John Ruskin* (1893), 234; quoted in DeVane, *Handbook,* 237.

gather some of the ideas for his poetry, as we have seen. They are useful to us in analysing the exact position of each of the religious monologues in Browning's thought. Each of the roles is intimately connected to one of the three great offices of Christ as Prophet, Priest, and King. In Browning the office of Christ as High Priest is seen as a poetic role in the Christ-types that he is portraying. The poet is the *vates*, and that is the link with the priestly function which Browning requires. Thus it is in a direct relation with the Incarnation that Browning can see these three roles, and so in the same relation he sees his own vocation as a poet, as early he had seen at the end of *Pauline*:

> . . . I shall live
> With poets, calmer, purer still each time, . . . but now
> I shall be priest and prophet as of old.   (1014–1019)

The close connection between *Cleon* and *Saul* is seen in the similarity of the themes that are treated no less than in the different attitudes that are taken by the monologuists. Even the incomprehensible suffering of Saul, the unknown meaning of his life, is related to the view that Browning had of the vain suffering of Empedocles. In *Saul* the suffering is given meaning, the agony is sublimated; in *Cleon* the same truth is presented, but the different context permits, even necessitates, a different conclusion.

Saul presented the vision of an Incarnate God; *An Epistle* dealt with an Eastern encounter with the objective reality of that truth; *Cleon* treated another aspect of the same subject, the conflict between Greece and Christianity; and the pattern is continued by the vision of the Incarnate God which is offered as an encounter with objective truth by the dying Saint John in *A Death in the Desert*.

Between the religious monologues published in *Men and Women* in 1855 (we shall leave our discussion of *Bishop Blougram's Apology*, published in the same volumes, until later) and those which appeared in *Dramatis Personae* in 1864, Browning had suffered the greatest blow of his life. Elizabeth Barrett Browning had died at Casa Guidi in Florence on June 29, 1861. Browning's intimate friend, W. W. Story wrote to Charles Eliot Norton an account of Browning's feelings shortly after his wife's death:

"The cycle is complete," as Browning said, looking round the room; "here we came fifteen years ago; here Pen was born; here Ba wrote her poems for Italy. She used to walk up and down this verandah in the summer evenings, when, revived by the southern air, she first began to enjoy her outdoors life. Every day she used to walk with me or drive with me, ... Last week, when we came to Florence, I said: 'We used, you know, to talk on this verandah so often—come and walk up and down once. Just once,' I urged, and she came to the window and took two steps on it. But it fatigued her too much, and she went back and lay down on the sofa—that was our last walk. . . . So the cycle was completed for us here, and where the beginning was is the end. Looking back at these past years I see that we have been all the time walking over a torrent on a straw. Life must now be begun anew—all the old cast off and the new one put on. I shall go away, break up everything, go to England, and live and work and write."[11]

To London he did go, and, there as DeVane says, "we find him reading such books as *Essays and Reviews*, Darwin's *Origin of Species*, Colenso's *Pentateuch*, Strauss's *Das Leben Jesu*, and Renan's *La Vie de Jésus*."[12] These made their contribution to *Dramatis Personae*, in particular affecting *A Death in the Desert* and *Caliban upon Setebos*.

A Death in the Desert was probably begun before Mrs. Browning's death, as another outgrowth of his thought coming from *Christmas-Eve and Easter-Day* and *Saul*, written in the main at Florence in 1860, or else in Brittany during 1862 and 1863, and then added to before publication in 1864. Browning was making his reply to the Higher Critics, constructing his own artistic defence of the authenticity of the Gospels on the basis of their personal validity, as he testified to Mrs. Orr: "The evidence of divine power is everywhere about us; not so the evidence of divine love. That love could only reveal itself to the human heart by some supreme act of *human* tenderness and devotion; the fact, or fancy, of Christ's cross and passion could alone supply such a revelation."[13] It has been a commonplace of Browning criticism to link *A Death in the Desert* with *Cleon* and *An Epistle*, and the connections must not be forgotten. All three poems stress the human need as well as the searching for Christianity, and all three have taken place after Christ's death. However, the death of St. John in the desert has also much in common with *Saul*. Saul's suffering condition may be contrasted with the dying thoughts of St. John, but the most striking parallels are

[11]Letter of W. W. Story to Charles Eliot Norton, August 15, 1861, printed in Henry James, *William Wetmore Story and his Friends* (Edinburgh, Blackwood), II, 64–6; quoted in Orr, *Life and Letters of Robert Browning*, in a note supplied by the revising editor, Sir Frederick G. Kenyon, 242, n. 1.

[12]*Handbook*, 281.

[13]Orr, "The Religious Opinions of Robert Browning," 879; in DeVane, *Handbook*, 297.

between St. John and David. David is the poet, the prophet, and is to be the king. This is the old trinity so familiar to Browning, representing love, knowledge, and power (*Paracelsus*) or what Is, what Knows, and what Does (*A Death in the Desert*). St. John is represented in *A Death in the Desert* as the author of the Gospel attributed to him, as well as the Epistles and the Apocalypse. Because St. John wrote a work of such lyrical and mystical beauty in the Fourth Gospel, Browning can assign him a place among the poets, for he possesses "the highest faculty that gives first rank"; he is a "Maker-see." Because of his vision of heaven in the Apocalypse, and in the poem because of his prophecy of the coming ages when even his own existence will be doubted by the higher critics, St. John is depicted also as the prophet. Finally, as one of the Apostles, as Bishop of Ephesus, and as a "warrior saint," St. John again parallels David's kingship over Israel as leader of the New Israel, the Christian community. That which in *Saul* had been vision is in the later monologue truth.

A Death in the Desert is close to *An Epistle* and *Cleon* in that each poem purports to be a written account in which the central character is able to express himself to his readers by means of a letter or manuscript. Such an indirect pattern is not part of the structure of *Saul*. If we were to link the Judaeo-Christian monologues as we did with the pagan monologues, *Cleon* and *An Epistle*, we should see a similar pattern emerging. Both *Saul* and *A Death in the Desert* have been linked with *Christmas-Eve and Easter-Day* in their genesis by DeVane, and we have noted some of the similarities in theme. Again the parallel in terms of poet-prophet-king is illuminative. David, the poet of the Psalms, had a prophetic vision of Christ, and is himself one of the ancestors of Christ. Christian tradition has persistently regarded him as an Old Testament type of Christ, not least in his role as king of Israel. St. John is, in Browning's view, the poet of the Gospel, a "Maker-see" in giving the vision of Christ to the future (and therefore a prophet), and one of the rulers in the kingdom of the New Israel, fulfilling the prophecy of Revelation 5:10: "And hast made us unto our God kings and priests: and we shall reign on the earth." *Saul* takes place in the pre-Christian era, but because of the visionary powers of David, redemption is seen to be possible in the future. The death of St. John takes place in the Christian era, but at a significant time as the last person dies who had experience of Jesus in the flesh. Both of these experiences are related so intimately to Christ because both are in the time-sequence of history that the Incarnation redeemed.

One of Browning's most important concepts, the doctrine of the three souls, is found in the second gloss on St. John's words in *A Death in the Desert*. This doctrine is seen by Browning as an analogy of the Trinity:

> This is the doctrine he was wont to teach,
> How divers persons witness in each man,
> Three souls which make up one soul: first, to wit,
> A soul of each and all the bodily parts,
> Seated therein, which works, and is what Does,
> And has the use of earth, and ends the man
> Downward: but, tending upward for advice,
> Grows into, and again is grown into
> By the next soul, which, seated in the brain,
> Useth the first with its collected use,
> And feeleth, thinketh, willeth,—is what Knows:
> Which, duly tending upward in its turn,
> Grows into, and again is grown into
> By the last soul, that uses both the first,
> Subsisting whether they assist or no,
> And, constituting man's self, is what Is—
> And leans upon the former, makes it play,
> As that played off the first: and, tending up,
> Holds, is upheld by, God, and ends the man
> Upward in that dread point of intercourse,
> Nor needs a place, for it returns to Him.
> What Does, what Knows, what Is; three souls, one man. . . .
>
> *A Death in the Desert* (82–103)

Here, in his most significant religious poem after *Christmas-Eve and Easter-Day*, Browning moves from his initial position of religious affirmation to belief in the Trinity. It is the Incarnation that is the root of the belief in the Trinity because that doctrine is the source of the analogy between the human and the divine, and it provides Browning with his basic pattern. Just as each of the souls has its own particular function but all make up the essential unity of man, so each of the Persons of the Trinity has his function, but all make up the unity of God. Furthermore, the analogy is made more complete by Browning in explaining the nature of the three souls and their relation to the Persons of the Trinity by the use of the three aspects that we have noted in

St. John, poet, prophet, and Apostle-bishop. The first soul, which uses the evidence of the senses, is the agent of human power, and this soul Browning describes as "what Does." The second (rational) soul uses both the mind and the senses, and is the agent of human wisdom, whose function Browning describes as "what Knows." Both of these souls seem to be limited in their function just as human power and human wisdom are limited. The third soul is the essential and vital part, using the functions of the other two souls as the agent of human love, designated as "what Is." This soul is seemingly unlimited in its capacity to love. Even the ironic reference to the attack on the Trinitarian analogy by the Higher Critics illustrates the theme:

> Go back, far, farther, to the birth of things;
> Ever the will, the intelligence, the love,
> Man's!—which he gives, supposing he but finds,
> As late he gave head, body, hands and feet,
> To help these in what forms he called his gods.
> First, Jove's brow, Juno's eyes were swept away,
> But Jove's wrath, Juno's pride continued long;
> As last, will, power, and love discarded these,
> So law in turn discards power, love and will.
>
> (411-19)

Each of these souls is located traditionally in a particular part of the body, according to the ancient physiologies which Browning seems to have followed. But Browning has also included another important means of understanding the nature of the Trinity. He is using the doctrine of analogy as a means of moving from the psychological nature of man to the nature of God.[14] We now have the complementary doctrines which balance one another in Browning's doctrine of the three souls. The Incarnation is the means of moving from the divine to the human level in the analysis of the three souls as types of the Trinity; and the analogical method (using the attributes of love, wisdom, and power) is the means of moving from the human to the divine level. Browning has only come to his use of analogy through the long development from *Pauline* through *Paracelsus* and *Sordello* to *Christmas-Eve and Easter-Day* and *Saul*. Thus elements from all these poems continue to be present in the treatment that Browning gives to the three

---

[14]For some of the background to these ideas of the three souls, and the analogy of the Trinity in man's faculties, see the appendix to chapter II.

souls. The doctrine tells us, as Browning wrote in *Paracelsus* (V), "What God is, what we are, what life is." By the use of analogy and the doctrine of the Incarnation, Browning has moved from faith in Christ alone to faith in the Trinity. His own analysis of human nature (the unified and yet tri-partite soul of man) tells him "what we are." Finally, his meditation upon the life of St. John, and especially his death, tells him "what life is," or at any rate, what life can be when it is lived to the fullest, in the light of full and perfect love, and in the constant presence of the eternal moment. That is the life of the saint, the artist, the poet.

When St. John in Browning's poem says that for him the life and death of Christ "—Is, here and now," he is making of the whole complex of Christ's action a moment in and out of time. That series of events which he witnessed, and then knew in thought, and then loved in contemplation, is an omnipresent and eternal moment; in that moment St. John apprehends "naught else" than the Incarnate Christ. He has experienced the Eternal made Man as Lazarus did, and the certainty of his knowledge is the blinding light of truth—the star which opens out on all sides, to employ Browning's favourite image for truth, and which is the whole world of experience for St. John:

> Then stand before that fact, that Life and Death,
> Stay there at gaze, till it dispart, dispread,
> As though a star should open out, all sides,
> Grow the world on you, as it is my world.
>
> (240–3)

David's vision in *Saul* is brought into the eternal present by Browning, "How love might be, hath been indeed, and is" in St. John's words, when the vision of David had become past event and present reality. But faith in the Christ as the Son of God remains as certain knowledge only to St. John; others are beset by the same (and necessary) attack on faith that Karshish suffered: doubt. There was no time in the Christian ages when faith was easy, for

> Already had begun the silent work
> Whereby truth, deadened of its absolute blaze,
> Might need love's eye to pierce the o'erstretched doubt.
>
> (319–21)

Even God's interjection of the supernatural into the natural order in a miracle, at first a proof of power, proved to be an embarrassment to faith; faith is not compulsive knowledge. St. John moves into his own visionary faculty as he explores the avenues of doubt. He foresees a Strauss-like attitude which finds in Christ the love and the power which we know in men and the world combined in myth. The myth is "true" in the sense that it is speaking about an eternal reality about man and his condition; it is myth in that the chronicle of the events is poetic myth, attached to the name of Christ. Then scientific power is examined as a projection of man's mind. Science says that the sun is driven by a force which it cannot explain, and the force is called a law. However, this law has not the faculties of power, love, and will which are evident in the ordered and systematic universe. The answer which Browning's St. John makes to these prophetically imagined assaults on the faith of the Incarnation is typically nineteenth-century:

> I say that man was made to grow, not stop. (424)

Here is our old friend, The Doctrine of Progress, newly baptized. It is placed in St. John's mouth with the meaning that man is mutable, but his mutations are part of the ordered scheme of providential nature. God controls the mutations of man, and these mutations are part of a development, enabling man to more and more fully apprehend God's revelation of himself at each stage of man's progress:

> This imports solely, man should mount on each
> New height in view; the help whereby he mounts,
> The ladder-rung his foot has left, may fall,
> Since all things suffer change save God the Truth.
> Man apprehends Him newly at each stage
> Whereat earth's ladder drops, its service done.
>
> (428-33)

Man is still able to doubt that there is love behind the power and the knowledge that are seen in the world. He knows that he loves, and desires to be loved, but how, asks Browning, introducing the striking image of the gutted lamp, can a man help one who

> Yet, owning his own love that proveth Christ,
> Rejecteth Christ through every need of Him?
> The lamp o'erswims with oil, the stomach flags
> Loaded with nurture, and that man's soul dies.
>
> (510-13)

The truth is too compulsive, so that it strangles that which it would feed. Yet man must strive for truth, and in the striving there lies a meaning for life. By striving man is able to exercise his will, his knowledge, and his love in the pursuit of truth, not the mere concealing, empirical fact. Such striving is characteristic of man in his distinctive place in nature, as a rational being, endowed with an immortal soul—not God, but having God's end to serve. Here man is to find his true progress; and the lamp, shining with the light of truth in the darkness of limited fact, is not gutted. The light of the lamp enables man to perceive everywhere the truth under a new aspect, and yet it is not wholly seen until man comes to his glory. St. John has followed the Way in his actions ("what Does"); he has known the Truth in the flesh ("what Knows"); he has lived the Life of love ("what Is") to the last, seeking still to pluck "the blind ones back from the abyss" in his last words. The Way, the Truth, and the Life have led St. John to his reward, for

> . . . now the man
> Lies as he lay once, breast to breast with God.

> (663–4)

But Browning's final comment upon St. John as the antitype of the Straussian nineteenth-century sceptic comes again in the important gloss on the account of St. John's death. Cerinthus muses and reads the gloss that while Christ was mere man (a gnostic doctrine, representing Strauss) he promised more than mere man could hope to fulfil. Thus Christ must be mad (disproved by the accounts, which nowhere give any ground for such a belief, as in the controversy recorded in John 10:20, 21) or a liar (which is unlikely, since so many would have had to be duped) or God. There can be no half-way stand with Christ, as Strauss was proposing in the myth theory, because he is either the "illimitable God, Or lost!" To Browning it is Strauss who is lost with Cerinthus; in them the flame of the lamp has been gutted; in the search for the truth they rejected truth through very need of it. Browning's answer to Strauss is in terms of incarnational Christology seen in the light of the Trinitarian theology that Browning has developed in the poem by the use of the analogy of human psychology.

A Death in the Desert formulates a complex pattern in Browning's poetry. It is a pattern that we have seen indicated before, because there are ample hints of it in the earlier poetry. Browning has forsaken the more strictly *dramatic* element in his dramatic monologues for the delights of casuistic exposition. To find the dramatic situation in *A Death in the Desert* one has to constantly remember that there are two fields of interest in the poem. The external dramatic device is the fact that St. John is hiding in the cave with his fellow Christians while a persecution is raging about them, threatening their existence at every moment. However, the situation is made more complex by the fact that the whole account exists in a manuscript, itself dictated to Phoebas by an unnamed narrator who is writing in prison before going to his martyrdom in the arena. Furthermore, there are marginal glosses on the manuscript which give further opinions. Browning does not appear to be far behind the semi-transparent mask of his *persona*, but the extreme contrivance of the dramatic events becomes confused in the maze of the internal situation. Here, in the speeches of St. John (and the contrast with them provided by Cerinthus' comments, and the explanations in the gloss), is the internal conflict, the relation between the doctrine of the three souls and the life of faith. But in all of the doctrinal exposition the structure of the poem disappears. If truth is the ultimate concern of the poem (including man's modes of apprehending the truth), then the poem's structure is not wholly devoted to that concern.

In the poem's thought, however, Browning has given considerable attention to one of the most important of his theories about human nature, the doctrine of the three souls, and that theory is to underlie the whole range of his poetry, as it had done previously from *Paracelsus* and even *Pauline*. But now the context is specifically Christian; Browning is clear about the analogical implications of the doctrine.

Despite the division of man into three souls, Browning still sees him as an essential unity. The point is important because it safeguards the effectiveness of the analogy with the Trinity on the one hand, and retains the value of each of the faculties in its own sphere on the other. Browning does not fall into the error of the faculty psychologists who would see a conflict between the warring powers of love and reason. Nor does Browning underestimate the value of knowledge; indeed, in the questing struggle to attain it is found life's meaning. But it is true that Browning denies the possibility *in this life* of perfect knowledge; it is essential to his doctrine of the three souls that man's knowledge *is* limited and imperfect. The search for more perfect knowledge is pursued through facts, certainly, but only contemplation of the facts can bring one to the truth that lies beyond and above mere fact. Knowledge has its role in the attainment of truth—and truth is the approach to beatific wisdom. Allied to Browning's theory of knowledge is a corollary related to certainty. Certainty destroys the meaning of the struggle for truth. Doubt is then seen as a valuable part of the quest and struggle. Doubt ensures the absence of certainty and demands a predicated imperfect knowledge. When imperfect knowledge is coupled with love, and when the resultant power is put into valuable action, man has found his true course, a progress towards God. The beast does not desire God; the angels are already in his presence; only to man is the desire possible; in the fulfilling of the desire man is realizing his real self, because only then is he doing that for which he was created:

> He is mere man, and in humility
> Neither may know God nor mistake himself; . . .
> Made to know that he can know and not more:
> Lower than God who knows all and can all,
> Higher than beasts which know and can so far
> As each beast's limit, perfect to an end,
> Nor conscious that they know, nor craving more;
> While man knows partly but conceives beside,
> Creeps ever on from fancies to the fact,
> And in this striving, this converting air
> Into a solid he may grasp and use,
> Finds progress, man's distinctive mark alone,
> Not God's, and not the beasts': God is, they are,
> Man partly is and wholly hopes to be.

> (572–88)

All three souls in man comprise a unity, but they are related further than that. The three actions, one of which each of the souls initiates and completes—doing, knowing, and being—are really summed up in the exercise of the highest function, that of being. The doing and the knowing are in no way inferior to being in their own spheres of action, but since being includes the former two, it is the crown and heart of man. Doing and knowing are less complete than being, and it is here that their inferiority lies. In the "being" of man both of the other functions are active. It is important to notice that in the being of man is also found the meaning of the moment. Doing, knowing, and being all occur in the moment; in the sudden shining light of the star of truth, in its momentary gleam, the moment of doing, knowing, and being gives meaning to man's existence. Perhaps all is made most clear when we remember that for Browning the most characteristic moment is the moment of revelation. It is then that two human souls can meet in understanding communion; it is then that the light of truth is most clearly perceived; it is then that an individual human life can receive its real meaning. Doing, knowing, and being are supremely united in the supreme moment of revelation, the Incarnation. Browning's own analogy of the three souls provides the *schema* for his synthesis. The Trinity is revealed in the Incarnation in all of its fulness; it is revealed in Unity; it is the moment which eternally is, giving meaning to all of the subsequent moments which more or less partake of its revelatory and eternal nature. In the Incarnation human souls can meet with God in understanding communion; in the Incarnation the light of truth is most clearly perceived; in the Incarnation human life has received its real meaning.

A Death in the Desert is most valuable for its statement in an oblique way of several crucial points in Browning's thought. Recognition of the tripartite structure of man's soul can never remove the necessity of action. The function of man's soul is to lead to right action, and right action in itself requires moral choice. Man's bodily needs are at once recognized, and the value of physical things is at once understood in relation to man's bodily needs. It is important that St. John should be made by Browning to say that man's spiritual needs are not so readily recognized; and the proper value of moral things is not fully understood. Man is to use the faculties of his unified soul to come to a more complete awareness of the proper value of moral things, and to use them in moral actions.

Two other religious poems, *Bishop Blougram's Apology* and *Caliban upon Setebos*, are not related in as direct a way to the life of Christ as the other monologues we have examined. But both poems grew out of Browning's religious interests and meditations, and they provide a neat set of contrasts whereby we come closer to completing our examination of Browning's religious attitude. *Bishop Blougram's Apology* is another of the by-products, if such it may be called, of the work that Browning did on *Christmas-Eve and Easter-Day*, having been written some time between 1850 and 1854. The references to Cardinal Wiseman (who provided Browning with some elements of a model) show the poem to have been written in part after Wiseman was created Archbishop of Westminster in October 1850. *Caliban upon Setebos* was written about ten years later, after the publication of Darwin's *Origin of Species* (November 1859), and was first published in *Dramatis Personae* (1864). *Bishop Blougram's Apology* first appeared in *Men and Women* in 1855.

Caliban upon Setebos is remote in time and space; it is far removed from the Incarnation, and presents a view of "natural theology in the island" rather than any form of revelatory religion. On the other hand, *Bishop Blougram's Apology* is set in the contemporary world, the present in time and space. Natural theology plays its part in the bishop's arguments, showing how the divine power and wisdom are present in the world, and are apparent to the natural quest. So it is with Caliban. He sees evidence of the power of the deity and of the knowledge of the deity. But that same deity is malignant, having created an imperfect world; there is no evidence of loving solicitude on the part of the deity. Bishop Blougram uses all of the means that are at his disposal to arrive at a more adequate conception of God. He uses doubt, art, objective truth, personal experience, and human love as instruments for the strengthening of faith.

Bishop Blougram is the poet, the man of artistic temperament who can appreciate a fine painting, a good sherry, and a neat phrase. The subtle handling of the arguments which Gigadibs presents to him is brilliant; he always starts from Gigadibs' rather naive position, and then weaves his web. The complexities of argument are handled with all of the skill, compression, and synthesis of the literary artist. By virtue of his office, the bishop shares the prophetic faculty which has been given to the Christian Church; he is living in the light of the Christian revelation, and that has illuminated his life and has restored his blinded vision. The bishop is a leader of men, a captain of souls, a Prince of the Church. In his own world, in fact, the bishop is a king, although he is thought by the hack-writer Gigadibs to be either a knave or a fool. The full contrasts in *Bishop Blougram's Apology* may be seen between the two characters of the poem, the one acting as the speaker, and the other, Gigadibs, the real controller of the poem's course acting as a *muta persona*. While Bishop Blougram is the poet-type, the prophet (even in anticipating Gigadibs' assumptions), and the "king," Gigadibs is at best a third-rate journalist, tempted into writing of his encounter with the great Blougram as the high point of his literary career. He is the model of all things dull, scarcely clever enough to see his own limitations. Counter-balancing Blougram's prophetic faculty is Gigadibs' spiritual blindness. He has never experienced revelatory brightness; he despises faith and distrusts the bishop. Instead of being a leader of men, Gigadibs is a slave to a morality which has no basis in his reason, to his reason which cannot be adequately followed in his experience, and to his experience which is limited by his own circumstances. In each of the three categories Gigadibs is at the opposite extreme to Blougram. He is in reality the same type of religionist that we find in Caliban, but he has gone further than Caliban in rejecting what he believed were the superstitious trappings of his forebears. He has even rejected the doubtful privilege of cherishing a natural theology. Caliban is also far removed from Blougram. He is the most prosaic personality, although Browning ironically has him speak some extremely well-modulated poetry and he has a far more active imagination than Gigadibs. He, like Gigadibs, is blind to the real nature of the divinity before which he cowers in fear. He is ahead of Gigadibs in that he recognizes the existence of a divinity; he is behind him in that he completely misunderstands it. Gigadibs has at least the opportunity of knowing the nature of God through revelation that was denied to Caliban, and the conclusion of *Bishop Blougram's Apology* tells us that the Bishop had scored a victory: Gigadibs is off to Australia, seeking, like St. Paul, to cultivate that which he had previously attacked, and all in the revelatory light of a study of the Gospel of St. John. Caliban remains a slave to the fear which rules his life; Gigadibs is able to escape from the serfdom of his life by exchanging the complete overlordship of reason for the rule of faith. In Cleon the poet-prophet-king trinity is distorted; in Gigadibs and Caliban, it is inverted. The poet in Caliban has become prosaic, and in Gigadibs the poet is replaced by a hack writer. Caliban's prophetic sense as well as Gigadibs' has become blind. The king of creation (which Caliban should be as a sort of "noble savage") is inverted in his situation, so that he emerges as a slave to his passions; Gigadibs, with the doubtful benefit of civilization, is a slave to his bourgeois code.

Browning in these two monologues is not dismissing reason as wholly inadequate; he is saying that reason *by itself* cannot be the sole guide to truth. Reason must be aided by all the other faculties of man, chiefly faith and love. Since Caliban has neither of these, he cannot reach the truth about the nature of God by his reason alone. Blougram is aware that his belief in something which cannot be "proved" empirically is outrageous to Gigadibs, but Blougram has transcended reason and come to faith, and combined it with the experience of love.

Caliban upon Setebos presents an anthology of pre-Christian theology, and Browning goes to great length to show that such theologies are not equivalent to the Christian essentials (as against the deists) and that all theologies are not natural as the projections of men's minds (as against the onslaught of nineteenth-century rationalism from the scientists, mythologizers, and sceptics). To Browning the concept of a God of wrath is pagan. He puts so much emphasis on the importance of divine love that he eliminates divine wrath, and almost all of divine judgment. Browning has put much of his stress on St. John as the Apostle of love in the Fourth Gospel, but he has not made much use of the wrathful implications in the scenes of judgment in the Apocalypse. Christ has replaced the God of wrath from the Old Testament with the God of love of the New Testament. Something of this attitude is seen in *Saul* where a large part of the poem is on a level that Browning would characterize as natural theology, but as the poem moves into David's vision of Christ, the natural theology gives way to revelation, and love comes into the new moral universe. David can be retained from the Old Testament as the prophetic type of Christ. In *Caliban upon Setebos* the god of wrath is to be appeased by sacrifice, to Browning an element of pagan belief too. He would carry such an attitude further, so that the Christian Atonement as a sacrifice is in some sense distasteful to him, and so the doctrine is quietly dropped from his poetry. The Atonement did appear in *Easter-Day*, and there there was something of the grandeur of classical picturings of the Last Judgment, but gradually the Atonement is ignored. Browning has no conception of the Atonement as the necessary completion of the offering of love that was begun in the Incarnation. The Incarnation is not to restore to man the place which he had lost through his original sin, or through his fallen state, or his propensity to sin; nor is the Atonement to carry away the debt of that sin, however one may wish to regard it. The Incarnation is not understood in terms of the Atonement for man's state; it is seen in terms of a psychological need for the fulfilment of finite man in an infinite expression of divine love.

Since Caliban had not enjoyed the light of the Christian revelation, he had never experienced the *moment* of revelation. He exists in a state of hatred, envy, and fear, a condition of spiritual darkness. It is not possible for him to emerge from that state except by divine grace, in theological terms, or except by the star-flash of divine love, in Browning's terms. For Caliban there is no synthesis, because there is no moment of insight. He seems to exist in an eternity of non-being where he can scarcely help being sub-human. He has little element of free choice in his life since his actions are coerced by the manifestations of the power and vindictiveness of Setebos. For Browning the man who has lost his choice has lost that which separates him from the beasts. He then acts solely for the gratification of his appetites. Caliban differs from the beasts themselves because he very fruitfully explores the depths of his imagination. He seems to come as close as he can to a Christian theology without the benefit of revelation, but he remains indisputably separated from its essential nature.

Blougram argues on the premises of Gigadibs for the first part of the poem, and makes a great show in relinquishing his prejudiced dogmas with those of the journalist:

> I mean to meet you on your own premise:
> Good, there go mine in company with yours!

> (171–2)

Blougram lives his life in the light of "The Way, the Truth, the Life," the same eternal moment of Christ's action that was reality to St. John. To Gigadibs such faith is a betrayal of the intellect, but Blougram counters with the argument that his waking life demands that he use all of his powers, "heart, head and hand," the same trinity that we find in *A Death in the Desert* denoting love, knowledge, and power. Blougram points out the sheer impossibility of the life of complete doubt; one must put one's faith in something. One must choose the life of faith to make sense of life. Now the shift comes to the bishop's own grounds for "We're back on Christian ground." He argues that as his doubt is great, his faith is greater. Thus his life is possible: "I live my life here; yours you dare not live." He does not have to point out to Gigadibs the cruel fact that if he does not live the life of intellectual doubt he is dishonest to himself. Gigadibs had come expecting the sensational, secure in his rational superiority over the bishop; he was to experience the moment of revelation in his encounter with the mind which the bishop was to roll out before him. The encounter was more than a little embarrassing, leading the "literary man" to play with his spoons and range the olive stones about the plate's edge. The bishop had offered some counsel, "Do then,—act away!", and in the light of his new experience Gigadibs acted by taking passage to Australia. Something had shaken Gigadibs' complacency and disturbed his self-sufficient reason, so much so that he left undone his "two points in Hamlet's soul unseized by the Germans yet." He who had never questioned his own position was pricked by the slightest bit of doubt. The bishop's "Suppose we die to-night" completes the web that he has so skilfully drawn. Gigadibs' death could give no meaning or stamp of value to his life. To arouse that bit of doubt was all of the Bishop's intention. It was as far from his mind to deliver a course in Christian doctrine to Gigadibs as it was to reveal his inmost self to the writer (or Browning's to reveal *himself* to the reader). Instead he is content to show Gigadibs some of the different facets of his own position, if it could be dignified by such a name. It is not Blougram who is on trial, but Gigadibs. Blougram's *apologia*[15] is right for the situation—it is its own justification as a sophistical argument. By means of it Gigadibs *is* shocked, severely to his intellectual core, and through his moment of doubt he can begin to value his momentary revelation.

Browning's collection of poems that made up *Men and Women* (1855) had an epilogue in the poem, *One Word More*, in which he dedicated the two volumes to Elizabeth Barrett Browning. He uses an artistic form that he was never to use again, a unique tribute to the beloved, as Dante had done in his painting, or Raphael in his sonnets. Browning is speaking *in propria persona*, and offers to his wife the dedication, even the consecration, of his knowledge and his art and his love. The mention of Dante and Raphael ties in the chief artistic themes of the volumes, and the linking of these with the poet's love for Elizabeth is symbolized in the moon-vision, reminding one of the earlier use of the image in *Christmas-Eve*, when he also acknowledged a great debt to his wife. Similarly the later volume, *Dramatis Personae* (1864), had its *Epilogue* uniting the themes of the book, in which the poet again speaks without the concealing mask. David and Renan are two of the speakers, and Browning is the third. *Gold Hair* had mentioned the "Essays-and-

---

[15]See F. E. L. Priestley's article on the structure and motivation of the casuistry, "Blougram's Apologetics"; cf. also C. R. Tracy, "Bishop Blougram," and Cardinal Wiseman's review of *Bishop Blougram's Apology*.

Reviews' debate" and "Colenso's words," and these are caught up in the differing views of David (the ritualistic) and Renan (the rational). Against these ideas are set Browning's own views in the poems of the volume, in *A Death in the Desert, Caliban upon Setebos,* and *Mr. Sludge, "The Medium."* All of these deal with contemporary religious issues. *Mr. Sludge* speaks bitterly against the spiritualists whom Browning so heartily disliked (a point of disagreement with his wife); Browning held to the position which he stated in *A Death in the Desert* that God would not use miracles to coerce faith now. Even Browning's philosophic faith, as enunciated in the often-quoted first stanza of *Rabbi Ben Ezra* was opposed to such a doctrine. Browning's optimism, as in the line "Trust God: see all, nor be afraid!", was a much more secure safeguard against the inroads of quack religion (as in *Mr. Sludge*) or secularism. The last stanza of the *Epilogue* states Browning's position, not substantially changed from that which he took with so much soul-searching fifteen years earlier in *Christmas-Eve and Easter-Day*:

> That one Face, far from vanish, rather grows,
> Or decomposes but to recompose,
> Becomes my universe that feels and knows!
>
> (XII, 99–101)

We may think of St. John's prayer, "Grow the world on you, as it is my world," and recognize again that Browning's universe is one which has a real place for feeling, for knowledge, and for love, all as experienced in the beloved "Face," ratified in man's heart, and lived in man's actions.

The pattern of the religious monologues that we have to discuss is now completed. We have seen the movement in Browning's religious thought from *Christmas-Eve* through in a continuous line to the last lines of the *Epilogue* of 1864. In it all the reality of the love of Elizabeth Barrett leads Browning in his religious quest. His pattern of triads came to full blossom in *A Death in the Desert* where Browning's faith in the Incarnation has led him to faith in the Trinity as he examined the impact of the Incarnation in different time-space relations in history. The Incarnation remains at this first crisis of history as the vertical line which transfixes experience and redeems it. Karshish and Blougram and Gigadibs have their own connection with Christ in a direct line of descent bringing the pattern up to the immediate present when the same principles have to operate that were revelatory in the "moment" of St. John. Cleon and Caliban have no ultimate connection with the Christ-line beyond the fact that they are not in it.

Browning saw in the history of civilization three critical periods, the era of the time of Christ, the Renaissance, and the nineteenth century. In *Men and Women* he examined the impact of the first two critical periods upon each other, for they are far from separated, and in *Dramatis Personae* he applied what he learned from the earlier volumes to the new critical period, the second half of the nineteenth century. It was critical for Browning himself, because he had lost the half of his life, in the person of Elizabeth, and the new orientation must have been difficult. All three of the critical periods are seen in the revelatory light of the first, since it is from that crisis that the others take their meaning. Browning's view of history is seen in the relation of the three periods; it was a relationship that he was to explore to the end of his days. A poem like *A Death in the Desert* can be in two critical periods at the same time, and the *Epilogue* shares the same ambiguity. In the Incarnation they have their significance, since what has happened exerts its influence on the present, and the present is always pushing forward into the future by means of its visionary powers. In the light of historical experience gained through what he has learned from the examples of the two critical periods of the past, Browning is able to face the present optimistically and with action.

APPENDIX

The classical physiology is gathered together by Burton in his *Anatomy of Melancholy*, where he tells us that the three spirits were located in the brain, the heart, and the liver, the three "noble parts," over which the heart is king, and by which a man chiefly is:

Spirit is a most subtle vapour, which is expressed from the *blood*, and the instrument of the soul, to perform all his actions; a common tie or *medium* betwixt the body and the soul, as some will have it; or, as Paracelsus, a fourth soul of itself. Melancthon holds the fountain of these spirits to be the *heart*; begotten there, and afterwards conveyed to the brain, they take another nature to them: Of these spirits there be three kinds, according to the three principal parts, *brain*, *heart*, *liver*; natural, vital, animal. The *natural* are begotten in the *liver*, and thence dispersed through the veins, to perform those natural actions. The *vital spirits* are made in the heart of the *natural*, which by the arteries are transported to all the other parts: if these *spirits* cease, then life ceaseth as in a *syncope* or swooning. The *animal* spirits formed of the *vital*, . . . give sense and motion to them all. (I.i.2.2)

... Of the *noble* there be three principal parts, to which all the rest belong, and whom they serve, *brain, heart, liver*; according to whose site, three regions, on a threefold division, is made of the whole body. As first of the *head*, in which the animal organs are contained, and brain itself, which by his nerves gives sense and motion to the rest, and is (as it were) a Privy Counsellor, and Chancellor to the *Heart*. The second region is the chest, or middle *belly*, in which the *Heart* as King keeps his Court, and by his arteries communicates life to the whole body. The third region is the lower *belly*, in which the liver resides as a hidden governor with the rest of those natural organs. ... (I.i.2.4)

Burton is simply making use of the common "scientific" heritage which explained the mechanics of the soul by means of physiological and psychological phenomena. It was understandable, then, that he should turn back to The Philosopher as his prime authority:

According to Aristotle, the soul is defined to be the Actual Being, the perfection or first act of an organical body, having power of life, which most Philosophers approve. ... Some therefore make one *soul*, divided into three principal faculties: others, three distinct *souls* ... : Paracelsus will have four *souls*, adding to the three granted faculties a *spiritual soul*. ... The common division of the *soul* is into three principal faculties, *vegetal, sensitive*, and *rational*, which make three distinct kinds of living creatures: *vegetal* plants, *sensible* beasts, *rational* men. How these three principal faculties are distinguished and connected, is beyond human capacity. ... (I.i.2.5)

Burton goes on to add Christian tradition to Greek learning, as he quotes the Fathers:

This *reasonable soul*, which Austin calls a spiritual substance moving itself, is defined by Philosophers to be *the first substantial act of a natural, human, organical body, by which a man lives, perceives, and understands, freely doing all things, and with election*. Out of which definition we may gather, that this *rational soul* includes the powers, and performs the duties of the two other, which are contained in it, and all three faculties make one *soul*, which is inorganical of itself, although it be in all parts, and incorporeal, using their organs, and working by them. It is divided into two chief parts, differing in office only, not in essence; the *understanding*, which is the *rational* power *apprehending*; the *will*, which is the *rational* power *moving*: to which two all the other *rational* powers are subject and reduced. (I.i.2.9)

Burton might have gone on to quote from St. Thomas Aquinas, who follows the same lines:

Considered under the form of a mixed body [a "mixed body" is composed of any combination of two or more of the four elements], it is in potency to a vegetative soul, for this sort of soul is the act of a body. In turn, the vegetative soul is in potency to a sensitive soul, and a sensitive one to an intellectual one. This process of generation shows: at the start of generation there is the embryo living with plant life, later with animal life, and finally with human life. After this last type of form, no later and more noble form is found in the order of generable and corruptible things. (*Summa Contra Gentiles*, III.22.7)

Similarily John Calvin agrees in the *Institutes*: "Nor am I disposed to quarrel with the view, that there are three principles of action—viz. sense, intellect, and appetite" (*Institutes*, I.xv.6). This same tradition, far from being the exclusive domain of the philosophers and theologians, is strong in English literature, appearing significantly in the writers of the seventeenth century. Thus Donne seems to be echoing the passage from St. Thomas as he writes: "*Man*, before hee hath his *immortall soule*, hath a *soule of sense*, and a *soule of vegetation* before that: This *immortall soule* did not forbid other *soules*, to be in us before, but when this *soule* departs, it carries all with it; no more *vegetation*, no more *sense* ..." (*Devotions*, XVIII). Earlier in the *Devotions* Donne had written of the three principal organs in the body in terms very similar to those of Burton:

And since the *Braine*, and *Liver*, and *Heart*, hold not a *Triumvirate* in *Man*, a *Soveraigntie* equally shed upon them all, for his *well-being*, as the foure *Elements* doe, for his very *being*, but the *Heart* alone is the *Principalitie*, and in the *Throne*, as *King*, the rest as *Subjects*, though in eminent *Place* and *Office*, must contribute to that, as *Children* to their *Parents*. . . . How little of a *Man* is the *Heart*, and yet it is all, by which he *is*. (*Devotions*, XI)

Again we may compare some sentences from Calvin to show the universality of these views, even though Calvin was introducing them in his *Institutes* to take issue with the primary governance of the will: ". . . The faculties of the soul are seated in the mind and the heart, [and so] let us now consider how far the power of each extends. Philosophers generally maintain that reason dwells in the mind like a lamp, throwing light on all its counsels, and, like a queen, governing the will . . ." (II.ii.2). In Sir Thomas Browne's *Religio Medici* we can perhaps expect to find record of the curious and out-of-the-way medical "philosophy." Browne refers to the Paracelsian theories of medicine which understand sulphur, mercury, and salt to be the three "hypostatical principles," the *tria prima*, and these three are also related to the three attributes of love, knowledge, and power by means of their association with the noble parts of the body:

And truly there goes a great deal of providence to produce a mans life unto threescore: there is more required than an able temper for those years; though the radical humour contain in it sufficient oyl for seventy, yet I perceive in some it gives no light past thirty: men assign not at all the causes of long life, that write whole Books thereof. They that found themselves on the radical balsome, or vital sulphur of the parts, determine not why Abel lived not so long as Adam. (I.xliii)

According to the alchemical theories, sulphur is connected with the heart (love, and in Browning, "what Is"), mercury with the brain (knowledge, "what Knows"), and salt or Browne's radical balsome with the liver (power, "what Does"). A table of magical or alchemical correspondences could be drawn up to illustrate the *tria prima* or Hypostatical Principles:

Category	The Tria Prima or Hypostatical Principles		
Tria Prima	Sulphur	Mercury	Salt
State:	oily	fluid	firm
Change of state:	burns	vaporizes	remains (ash)
Alchemical equivalent:	resin	arcanum	balm (balsam)
Element:	fire (& air)	water	earth
Realm of existence:	celestial	astral	visible, tangible
Mode of existence:	energy	spirit	mass
Seat in man:	heart	brain	liver
Physiology:	soul	intellect	body
Psychology:	feeling	thinking	willing
Attribute:	love	knowledge	power
Quality:	goodness	truth	beauty
Trivium:	rhetoric	logic	grammar
Human learning: (philosophy)	divine (theology)	natural (mathematics)	human (law)
Sphere of influence:	ethics	science	art
Type:	saint	scholar	artist

That Browning himself knew something of the *tria prima* is evident because he uses some material from Melchior Adam's *Vita Germanorum Medicorum* in his own notes to *Paracelsus*. Part of Adam's account is devoted to Paracelsus' teaching on medical, alchemical, and psychological subjects, and the relevant passage is quoted in DeVane's *Handbook* (53–4), where the three basic principles are mentioned. These principles provided Browning with the material to set up a complete set of correspondences and relationships which would be useful to him in his poetical and theological patternings. Browning applied what he learned from Paracelsian alchemy about the *tria prima* to his own meditation on human psychology and what he knew from traditional medicine. These correspondences were combined with earlier aesthetic theories (from *Sordello* and *An Essay on Shelley*). Thus the first or lowest rank of poet is purely descriptive (and so is related to the attribute of power, the Person of God the Father, the type of the king, and the mineral of salt). The second rank of poet tells the quiddity of what he has seen (and is related to knowledge, the Holy Spirit, the prophet, and mercury). The third or highest poet gives the gift of seeing to the rest of mankind (and so is related to love, the Son, the poet-priest-saint, and sulphur). With the exception of the mineral correspondences, all of these relationships are presented in that order in *A Death in the Desert*, and it is Browning's characteristic order.

Browning's use of the attributes of the Trinity, and their relation to the soul as well as to the rest of creation is wholly traditional and orthodox. It is more than likely that Browning knew the famous *Bridgewater Treatises*, "On the Power, Wisdom, and Goodness of God, as manifested in the Creation," which were published between 1833 and 1840. These writings had a great effect upon the popular imagination, and show that the subject was common enough in England several decades before Browning developed his full theory. Browning probably also knew Donne's use of the tripartite division of the body and the ascription of power, knowledge, and love to the Trinity from the Donne in his father's library:

> O Blessed glorious Trinity,
> Bones to Philosophy, but milke to faith,
>   Which, as wise serpents, diversly
> Most slipperinesse, yet most entanglings hath,
>   As you distinguish'd undistinct
>   By power, love, knowledge bee,
> Give mee a such selfe different instinct,
> Of these let all mee elemented bee,
> Of power, to love, to know, you unnumbered three.
>
> ("The Trinity," from *A Litanie*)

The concept was common to men of letters, appearing even in such secular places as George Peele's first play, *The Arraignment of Paris*. This play, ending so extravagantly with its tribute to Elizabeth, was performed before the Queen by the Children of the Chapel in 1581. Paris is to judge which of the goddesses is to receive the golden ball, the emblem of beauty. To tempt him, Juno offers power, Pallas offers knowledge, and Venus offers love, but to end the contest, Diana enters and presents the prize to Elizabeth. Here all of the attributes are showered upon the Queen in the courtly love tradition. But the court of England, for all its exalted tradition, remained the merest shadow of the court of heaven. Calvin draws us soberly back to the true archetype:

"The carnal mind, when once it has perceived the power of God in the creation, stops there, and, at the farthest, thinks and ponders on nothing else than the wisdom, power, and goodness, displayed by the Author of such a work . . ." (*Institutes*, I.xvi.1).

The ascription of the three attributes of love, knowledge, and power to the three Persons of the Trinity may be traced back to the treatise *De Trinitate* of St. Augustine. In that work, Augustine bases his argument on an analogy with his psychological theory of the powers of the mind. Augustine begins with his statement of the doctrine in the *Confessions*, where he distinguishes between Being, Knowing, and Willing, as the three distinctive faculties of man:

I could wish that men would but consider these three things that are in themselves, . . . namely, to Be, to Know, and to Will. For indeed I am, and I know, and I will. I am, both knowing and willing. I know myself both to be and to will. And I am willing both to be and to know. Let him therefore that can reach to it, comprehend in these three, how inseparable is life. . . . (XIII. xi.12)

Here is the essence of Browning's distinction among "what Does," "what Knows," and "what Is." In his treatise, *De Trinitate*, Augustine develops the connection between the faculties of man and the three Persons of the Trinity:

In these three, when the mind knows itself and loves itself, there remains the trinity, mind (= will), love, knowledge; and this trinity is not confounded by any commingling, although they are each severally in themselves, and mutually all in all, or each severally in each two, or each two in each. Therefore all are in all. For the mind certainly is in itself, since it is called mind in relation to itself; although it is called knowing, or known, or knowable, relatively to its own knowledge; although as loving, or loved, or lovable, it is referred to the love with which it loves itself. . . . Thus these things are severally in themselves. But so they are in each other, because the mind that loves is *in* love, and love is *in* the knowledge of him that loves, and knowledge is *in* the mind that knows. . . . And so there is a kind of image of the Trinity in the mind itself, and the knowledge of it, which is its offspring, and love as the third, and these three are one, and one substance. (IX.v.8; IX.xii.18)

Augustine relates the image of God which is impressed upon the mind (which is another name for soul to him) to the faculty of memory. When we will to recall anything to the mind, we recall that which we truly love when we remember most accurately. The mind thus recalls most supremely when it recalls the image of God which is impressed upon the soul by the power, love, and wisdom of God in creation:

We have urged those who demand a reason on such subjects to observe and understand the "invisible things" of God, so far as they may, by "the things that are made" (Rom. i, 20), and especially by the rational or intellectual creature which is made after God's image; through which glass, so to speak, they might discern as far as they could, if they could, the Trinity which is God, in our memory, understanding, will. And if anyone alertly explores these three things as by nature divinely appointed in his mind, and remembers by memory, contemplates by understanding, embraces by love, how great that thing in his mind is whereby even the eternal and immutable nature can be recollected, beheld, desired, that man assuredly finds an image of that supreme Trinity. . . . (XV.xii.42)

These three things, memory, understanding, and love, are mine, not their own; neither do they do what they do for themselves, but for me; or rather I do it through them. For it is I who remember by memory, understand by understanding, love by love. . . . By all these three things it is I who remember, I who understand, I who love, I who am neither memory, nor understanding, nor love, but who have them. These three things can therefore be expressed as by one person, which has these three, but is not itself these three. In the simplicity, however, of that supreme Nature, which is God, although there is one God, yet there are three Persons, the Father and the Son and the Holy Ghost. (XV.xxiii.43)

Faith in St. Augustine's system, when it is fortified by hope and love, refers to the things that are eternal, which is the enjoyment of the Trinity for ever. Faith, although it refers to eternal things yet is in itself a temporal thing, dwelling in time in the hearts of believers, and by it a man is able to will, to know, and to love the Trinity whose image he perceives through the glass of his soul. By faith the classical virtues are christianized, and have their own place in the scheme of salvation: "The virtues themselves, whereby in this temporal and mortal life men live prudently, bravely, temporately, and justly, are not true virtues, unless they are referred to that same faith, temporal though it is, which leads on nevertheless to things eternal" (XIV.i.3). All of Augustine's thought is caught up into his concept of the two cities, Babylon, the terrestrial city of damnation, and Jerusalem, the celestial vision of peace. Jerusalem is the work of the Trinity, and by patterning our doing, knowing, and loving on the will of the Trinity, we may attain to the heavenly city which is our true end:

. . . The whole Trinity is revealed to us in the Creation. In this, too, is the origin [cf. power], the enlightenment [cf. knowledge], the blessedness [cf. love] of the holy city which is above among the holy angels. For if we inquire whence it is, God created it; or whence its wisdom, God illumined it; or whence its blessedness, God is its bliss. It has its form by subsisting in Him; its enlightenment by contemplating Him; its joy by abiding in Him. It is; it sees; it loves. In God's eternity is its life; in God's truth its light; in God's goodness its joy. (*The City of God*, XI.24)

Browning's pattern of thought may be traced back to St. Augustine's, and it may be quickly seen that the patterns fit exactly. Browning has applied the pattern to his examination of the aesthetic activity of the poet engaged in creation. The pattern, a consistent one throughout Browning's life, shows love to be the basic faculty, and the Incarnation to be the central mystery. Both of these are means of approaching the mystery of the Trinity, love providing the way of analogy, and the Incarnation the way of revelation in the complex of history.

AESTHETIC UNITY: POETRY AND ART

... lyrics with more music and painting than before,
so as to get people to see and hear. ...
    (Browning, Letter to Milsand, February 24, 1853)

    ... What's come to perfection perishes.
Things learned on earth, we shall practise in heaven:
Works done least rapidly, Art most cherishes.
    (*Old Pictures in Florence*, XVII, 130–2)

I. THE MONOLOGUES ON PAINTING

In the religious monologues of the two great works of his mid-life Browning was concerned primarily with the effect of the birth of Christ upon the lives of men. The effect in some of the poems was carried on to Browning's own times, to show how it strikes a contemporary. On the other hand, the monologues concerned with art are set in the second great period of crisis in the history of the world, the Renaissance. But the "Renaissance monologues," as they are sometimes called, have their relevance only as they look back to the first great crisis, and look ahead to say something important to the present age. *Cleon* showed Browning's interpretation of the failure of Hellenism in not recognizing the Messiah. The rejection of Christianity by the Greeks had occurred in the first crisis of civilization. The Greek world with all of its cultural attainments and philosophical pre-eminence had rejected the offering of the Jewish world. History passed the lamp of Greek wisdom, burning somewhat less brightly, to be sure, to Rome, and there, mixed with Christianity, it began to shed a little clear light.

The success of Roman civilization in passing the intellectual activity of Greece on to the Renaissance came from the stress which Christianity placed upon the role of the individual, his right to immortality, and his responsibility before God. But after the first Christian efflorescence, Christianity was pushed underground by waves of persecutions, and these were followed by what Browning viewed as the dark ages. The Renaissance witnessed several events: a rebirth of the place of the individual in society (and so in art), a new appreciation of classical culture (baptizing much of it into Christian use), and the first conflicts of an oncoming age of science with an age of belief. It is especially in the art of the Renaissance, its painting and its music, that the meeting of forces can be felt; Browning is concerned to show that what he learned from interpreting that meeting of forces should be applied to the present.

Browning reflects on the nature of art as seen through a series of important artists, and his reflection operates in two ways. He persistently maintains that the art and the artist of the Renaissance offer an analysis of the present. Secondly, the art of the Renaissance can do this only because it shares, along with the present, in the eternal "now" of the first great crisis of history, the Incarnation. The Renaissance can gather together the thoughts of men about the artistic activity (itself analogous to the activity of God in creation and redemption, as Browning was aware) and can present it to future generations as additional illumination of the central truth which comprehends all art. The difference between the theological and the poetic enterprises comes from the nature of the activity. The poet is creating a work of art, a poetic structure at once strikingly personal and objectively evocative—not life itself, but an artistic commentary on life. Here is the same connection with reality that we find in musical activity, the ordered pattern, thoroughly mathematical, of notes on the page of music which, when transplanted into their own reality in the heard sound, conjure up in the listener the same personal and evocative response that the pattern of sound and meaning calls from the poem. Theology involves an examination of the ground of being that is common to all modes of discourse, although it is quickly seen that painting, music, and poetry *are* or exist in different ways. It is in this sense that aesthetic theory can interact with theological presentation, and a new light can be shed on the one discipline by the illumination and the wisdom of the other. Thus Collingwood's great definition of art as "aesthetic pattern in significant form" can have even profounder meaning than is at first apparent when it is applied to Browning's poetry on painting and music as essentially ontological inquiries into the nature of life. "Aesthetic pattern" must refer to the execution of the work of art, while "significant form" is more directly related to the ontology of the work of art. The form of art refers to its location in the field of reality, and, in that the work of art *is*, it partakes of the nature of God whose chief characteristic is being, as St. Thomas (*ipsum esse subsistens*) and Browning (what Is) agree. In giving the work of art its form, the artist is primarily the creator, and it is in this activity that his work is analogous to the activity of God. To make this connection between painting and theology clearer, Eric Gill, in his *Christianity and Painting* comments that "man by his free will is capable of original creation, and a work of art is such by reason of its original form."[1] By "original form" (cf. Collingwood's "significant form") Gill means what is "essentially a matter of order, it is the 'splendor formae' of St. Thomas, it is the shining out of Being, it is the thing called beauty."[2] Browning's examination of the nature of beauty is an inquiry into the meaning of life. His poems on art and artists could only be contemplated after his theological position had been clarified. Only when he knew something of the implications of an incarnational theology from *Christmas-Eve and Easter-Day* could he explore the implications of the Christian art of the Renaissance. Browning's choice of Christ ("I choose here!") is an acknowledgment of the presence to Browning of the Christ whose ontological nature is "the shining out of Being." So the examination of the artist (both the artist of the Renaissance in the monologues and Browning's own development as a poet) is an examination of the ground and nature of Being. The theologian, raising and purifying his speculation up to the metaphysical notion of being, finally arrives at the most hidden and the most revelatory of all acts, the act-of-being; and similarly the creative artist, purifying his creation of all direct and immediate self-revelation of the act-of-being, provides us with a visible image or sensation or analysis of it that corresponds to what its intuition is in the mind of the metaphysician.[3] Browning had come to know the act of begotten responsive

[1] *Christianity and Painting*, as quoted in Gilson, *Painting and Reality*, 296, 301; cf. Donald Davie, "Two Analogies for Poetry," *Listener* (April 5, 1962).

[2] Gilson, *Painting and Reality*, 300.

[3] Gilson, *Painting and Reality*, 50.

love, and in *A Death in the Desert* he tried to formulate the genesis of that act and that love from a Trinity of Persons. Browning's knowledge of God's self-revelation came in an aesthetic form. The Renaissance monologues on art are the aesthetic response that the revelation of God brought to Browning.

Browning knew that the aesthetic experience requires time. Time is needed for the experience to develop in the artist; time is required in the writing or painting of the experience; and time is required in the appreciation of the experience by the reader or viewer or listener. For his concourse of aesthetic experiences, Browning chose the Renaissance as a period about which the world had long had time to meditate. His own poetic sensibilities found there a convenient and harmonious frame of expression. Finally, Browning found in the Renaissance what he needed to fit his philosophic and theological interests. The Renaissance is a period of crisis to Browning, and the crisis demands an answer. Just as the time of the Incarnation demanded an answer to the question, "What think ye of Christ?" so the Renaissance was asking, in Browning's mind, "What think ye of Art?", and the two questions are really the same one seen in different aspects. They demand an answer in terms of what man expects from life. The Renaissance monologues cannot, therefore, be considered as poems which have a totally different subject-matter from the rest of Browning's poetic activity. They are connected intimately with the rest of the poetry both internally in the use of the same themes in poetry, religion, and art, and externally in the time sequence of history that Browning saw extending in a direct line from the Incarnation to the Renaissance, and on to the last critical period of experience, the Victorian era.

Browning's first essay into the culture and art of the Renaissance, *My Last Duchess*, is also one of his greatest. The duke is negotiating for a new duchess, and in the course of the monologue reveals some of the intricacies of his austere character. The poem is not merely an examination of the social situation where the bride is regarded by the duke as another of his almost priceless *objets d'art*. It is also a serious moral study of social motivation. The duke has all the *power* of a Machiavellian prince; he has the *knowledge* of a man of culture, a patron of the arts, literature, sculpture, and painting. But Browning shows that these qualities are not redeemed by the leaven of *love*. The duke's attitude towards art is a selfish delight in mere possession. From his attitude towards his paintings we know that that is also his attitude towards life. He wishes to possess the next duchess as a work of art in his already extensive collection. Mere possession rather than aesthetic enjoyment ministers to his pride which emerges even through the shell of the duke's coldly formal courtesy. The individual who should be redeemed has lost his life-giving link with the source of life. Time for the duke is a succession of possessed fragmentations, not a moment of visionary unity in which he can see his life in terms of art, or his art in terms of life. Browning's duke is in the same position with respect to the Incarnation as Cleon, and the two characters are neat complements.

My Last Duchess was first published in *Dramatic Lyrics* (1842) and its companion piece is naturally *The Bishop Orders His Tomb at St. Praxed's Church*, which appeared in *Hood's Magazine* in 1845 and in the same year was reprinted in *Dramatic Romances*.[4] Ruskin thought that the poem breathed the "Renaissance spirit,"[5] and it is the same spirit that informs *My Last Duchess*. The duke and the bishop are poured from the same mould; both have the same morality (or lack of it); the bishop's learning is somewhat more pedantic; both delight in the possession of material goods as objects of personal pride and means of personal immortality. Both are seen in a critical life-moment, the one as he contracts to acquire a new duchess, the other at the point of death. In the moment the whole expanse of each life is seen, the delights, vanities, and characteristics. Neither duke nor bishop is able to face the point of time, the critical moment in each life (and also the critical period in which each lived) by wedding love to power and knowledge.

[4]Browning was aware of the upsets that had been occurring at Oxford in the heat of the Tractarian movement. In 1841 Newman had published his *Tract XC*; in 1842 it was condemned by his bishop; in 1843 Newman published a retraction of all that he had said against the Roman Church, and followed this in 1844 by writing his *Essay on the Development of Doctrine*. In 1845, in October, Newman was received into the Roman Church, a matter of the most intense interest to all England. Browning was well aware of the opportunity that was presented to him, and published his *Bishop* when the press was full of the controversy. DeVane mentions (*Handbook*, 166) a letter sent to F. A. Ward, the sub-editor of *Hood's Magazine*, in which Browning says, ". . . I pick it out as being a pet of mine, and just the thing for the time—what with the Oxford business. . . ." Browning saw that his *Bishop* could say something to an aroused national interest, but its message was not one of love. Here is one more example of Browning's application of a period of historic crisis to the present age.

[5]"I know of no other piece of modern English, prose or poetry, in which there is so much told, as in these lines, of the Renaissance spirit,—its worldliness, inconsistency, pride, hypocrisy, ignorance of itself, love of art, of luxury, and of good latin" (in DeVane, *Handbook*, 167–8).

We should not be surprised at this serious moral defect; Browning had not yet come to write *Christmas-Eve and Easter-Day*. Indeed, in 1845 Browning was struggling with the fragment of *Saul* which he could not adequately complete until the experience of the 1850 poems had taught him about the Incarnation. So it is with *My Last Duchess* and *The Bishop Orders His Tomb*, since both are fragments of the unified picture of the Renaissance that Browning could present after the solidification of his religious experience. Neither the bishop nor the duke has learned to live the life of significant action (cf. the stationary inaction of the Saul of the first version), but each has taken transient delight in the appetitive and intellectual faculties of man at the expense of his spiritual faculty. A Renaissance ecclesiastic orders his tomb, and a Renaissance prince orders his wife, but these are not meant by Browning to be studies in the nature of sacred and profane love. They are instead partial examinations of the partially grotesque. The grotesque in Browning has frequently been noted, but it is not generally observed that the grotesque is caused by a defect in respect to love.

Browning uses his typical approach to a critical period when he comes to a serious study of the Renaissance. His method is to deal with some aspect of history before he presents his more complete synthesis. He had used the same method in the historical approach of *Saul*, but he needed the personal experience of *Christmas-Eve and Easter-Day*. Now in coming to the Renaissance he uses *Pictor Ignotus*, but he still needs the warmth of *Christmas-Eve* to impart love. Browning is not writing about art history, but about the aesthetic experience of art as art, and, more important to him, of art as life.

Pictor Ignotus, published in *Dramatic Romances* in 1845, was the first of Browning's poems which dealt with his interpretation of the history of Italian painting in the Renaissance. More particularly, he was interested in the development of art-forms, style, subject-matter, treatment, and the whole *métier* which characterized the movement from the fourteenth to the sixteenth centuries. The *Pictor Ignotus* is a painter-unknown, one without a name, without distinguishing characteristics which would single him out from among the others. In developing his other-worldly asceticism and humility, the painter has lost the nature of Christian individuality. But the artist is well aware of the fact that he is a little old-fashioned. He has no patience with his fellows who paint "each face obedient to its passion's law" since he can do that too. Instead he chooses to leave the individualized passions, the specific portraits of people, for the coming generation:

> . . . I paint
> These endless cloisters and eternal aisles
> With the same series, Virgin, Babe and Saint,
> With the same cold calm beautiful regard. . . . (58–61)

Here is the artist who produces the required religious altar-piece, conforming in every detail to the formalistic and symbolic language of design, colour, and subject which his medium and patron required. Browning sees in this type of art (and life) the ennui ("my heart sinks, as monotonous I paint") which can never give rise to living art. It is a sterile mediaeval equivalent to modern mediocre mass-production. The teaching of the Incarnation about the ultimate and absolute value of the unique was a forgotten characteristic of life and art. The importance of time as the realm of redemption instead of the passive quietude of waiting for the bliss of heaven was ignored. Browning's *Pictor Ignotus* shows the effect of this kind of idealism upon art and life, but his analysis of art history is only partially accurate if we are to follow an art historian like Huizinga in his *The Waning of the Middle Ages*. While Browning and Huizinga may disagree in the basic causes of the decline of the art of the Middle Ages, both agree in a much more important area: that it was philosophical and theological and aesthetic considerations (which were involved in the whole approach to life) that were at the root of the changes from the Middle Ages to the Renaissance. Along with the falling off of symbolic thought in favour of intricate elaboration, Huizinga also discusses the effects of realism:

This tendency to reduce all things to a general type has been considered a fundamental weakness in the mentality of the Middle Ages, owing to which the power to discern and describe individual traits was never attained. Starting from this premise, the well-known summary of the Renaissance as the coming of individualism would be justified. But at bottom this antithesis is inexact and misleading. Whatever the faculty of seeing specific traits may have been in the Middle Ages, it must be noted that men disregarded the individual qualities and fine distinctions of things, deliberately and of set purpose, in order to always bring them under some general principle. This mental tendency is a result of their profound idealism.[6]

The idealism of the unknown painter is what Browning is picturing in

[6] *The Waning of the Middle Ages*, 215.

his poem. He will proceed in other poems to examine painters of the *quattrocento* who are "modern" in their attitude to life and art. Browning saw in them a greater appreciation of the intimate connection that he too saw between life and art. Life, if it is to be creatively valuable, has to be artistic in some way. It has to have an appreciation of the value of the unique individuality of each element of reality, an appreciation that Browning had learned from the Incarnation. Huizinga delineates some of the connections between life and art that Browning was seeking to examine at the close of the Middle Ages:

Art in those times was still wrapped up in life. Its function was to fill with beauty the forms assumed by life. These forms were marked and potent. . . . The task of art was to adorn all of these concepts [religious, chivalric, courtly] with charm and colour; it is not desired for its own sake, but to decorate life with the splendour which it could bestow. Art was not yet a means, as it is now, to step out of the routine of every-day life to pass some moments in contemplation; it had to be enjoyed as an element of life itself, as the expression of life's significance. Whether it served to sustain the flight of piety or to be an accompaniment to the delights of the world, it was not yet conceived as mere beauty. . . . We should add that the love of art for its own sake did not originate in an awakening of the craving for beauty, but developed as a result of superabundant artistic production. In the treasuries of princes and nobles, objects of art accumulated so as to form collections. No longer serving for practical use, they were admired as articles of luxury and of curiosity; thus the taste for art was born which the Renaissance was to develop consciously.[7]

This is the point of departure in the history of aesthetics that Browning uses for his portraits of the duke and the bishop. The rise of humanism, phoenix-like from the ashes of the Middle Ages, brought its dangers of an increasing secularism, it is true, but Browning is trying to show that the values which were cherished by the new painters of the *quattrocento* were valuable in art because they had direct reference to value in life. The Incarnation put an ultimate stamp of value on human life, Browning argues, which would extend the implications of the Incarnation, not into the realm of dead saints, but among living men. Artists, who in the terms of the *Essay on Shelley* have "simultaneous perception of Power and Love in the absolute, and of Beauty and Good in the concrete," are supremely well equipped to extend the implications of the Incarnation. To Browning, some of the old painters of the Renaissance were such artists. He has tried to show in his poems on art that the transition from the mediaeval mind to the modern mind (as

[7]*Ibid.*, 244.

typified in the Renaissance) was a shift in the patterns and values of art, and that means for Browning a shift in the patterns and values of life.

Browning's use of the Florentine artists to express his views of the historical process was obvious not only because it was easier to see the process in Italy, but also because Browning was familiar with the paintings and painters of Florence; he studied them (as his use of Vasari indicates) and collected them himself. He saw in Italy the examples of painting which never lost the close connection with the antique spirit of classical art (harmony and simplicity, as Huizinga shows[8]), and yet could grow in the fresh air and liberty of Christian humanism. *Pictor Ignotus* admirably shows that Browning was aware of inconsistencies and misfits in the historical process of transition which was not an immediate reversal of aim and value. *Pictor Ignotus* indicates the direction that Browning's mind is moving in in his analysis of the historical process. It is an attempt at initial definition of difference between the mediaeval and modern spirits. Later poems will come to more definite conclusions which will be possible when the necessary references for them in the theological thought of Browning have been made secure. Browning knows that in the *chronos* of history the Renaissance stands out as a significant "season" of judgment. It is a *kairos*, a "time-with-content," no less than the time when the Kingdom was first declared to be at hand. It is the time when the significant opportunity occurs that had been prepared by providential arrangement. Man is to find in the Incarnation of love the means of coming to the redemption of the time.

Ten years after the first of Browning's poems on art appeared, the second series came to the public view in *Men and Women* (1855). These two volumes included *Fra Lippo Lippi, Andrea del Sarto, Old Pictures in Florence, A Grammarian's Funeral, A Toccata of Galuppi's*, and *Master Hugues of Saxe-Gotha*. Browning's aesthetic views on the Renaissance and the eighteenth century are contained in these poems, views which

---

[8]"The transition from the spirit of the declining Middle Ages to humanism was far less simple than we are inclined to imagine it. Accustomed to oppose humanism to the Middle Ages, we would gladly believe that it was necessary to give up the one in order to embrace the other. . . . In Italy the problem of humanism presents itself in a most simple form, because there men's minds had ever been predisposed to the reception of antique culture. The Italian spirit had never lost touch with classic harmony and simplicity. It could expand freely and naturally in the restored forms of classic expression. The *quattrocento* with its serenity makes the impression of a renewed culture, which has shaken off the fetters of mediaeval thought, until Savonarola reminds us that below the surface the Middle Ages still subsist." (*Waning of the Middle Ages*, 323.)

informed his attitude to poetry and life throughout his career until *Asolando* and the *Parleyings* summarized his life's estimate of their value.

In the period after *Christmas-Eve and Easter-Day* Browning developed the full scope of his *persona* in the monologues on religion and art. The *persona* has attained a unique status in Browning's thought analogous to the position of Christ. The *persona* is very carefully selected to represent just what Browning is trying to say in each situation. He is himself the symbol, the "fleshification," the incarnation, if one wishes, of Browning's idea. The *persona* is speaking (or reading or writing) to an audience of one or more people in circumstances which have in them the summation of a set of experiences, the succession of *chronoi* which the *persona* has witnessed; and the whole movement of thought is governed by the feelings of both the speaker and the listener. But the dramatic monologue is really a reflective poem in which the *persona*, meditating on the dramatic situation (a *kairos*), has to come to some kind of Christ-like solution which will redeem the time. He passes through a trial or conflict and at the end of the monologue can see with unusual clarity the implications of the thought and action of the poem. The speaker ruminates on the situation, on what led up to it, and on what lies in the future (like the times of reflection in Christ's life when the implications of the whole pattern of redemption are seen, as in the temptations in the wilderness before his preaching, and above all in the meditation in Gethsemene before the Passion). The reflections and aspirations of the speaker (and Browning's own thought) develop easily out of the matter of the poem and yet remain an integral part of it. The poem thus seems to be the ordering of the poet's own experiences and the voicing of his own opinions and prejudices. By means of the dramatic situation the poet is able to probe not only the character, psychology, philosophy, religion, and personality of the *persona*, but also the significant things which the poet sees in contemporary society, both his own and that of the poem. The *persona* in Browning has become not only the poetic type, but the symbol of an age or a civilization, the reality of the Incarnation in the mediate form of the human word present to each generation. The *personae* of *Men and Women*, Fra Lippo, Andrea, Galuppi, Hugues, and the rest, have assumed, each in his particular, and perhaps partial way, that status.

Fra Lippo Lippi begins *in medias res* in a dramatic situation where we find illustrated a pattern of history, conflicts between two views of life and art, and Browning's estimate of the life and work of Fra Lippo Lippi. In the monologue history and the historical pattern are represented in the figure of the artist. He is an example of the early Italian *quattrocento* and so is in conflict with the Prior who is of an earlier era. The differences between the thought of the Middle Ages and the Renaissance are illustrated in these two men. In art the Prior wishes to represent the world as perfected—the image of the ideal—those things which show the aspirations of the soul towards God; the artist wishes to paint life as it is. Here are two different views of the Incarnation. The former sees man's salvation as coming from an ascetic imitation of the life of Christ (the monastic ideal of the counsels of perfection); while the latter adopts a "realistic" view that man is a sinner living in a sinful world, and that he has to be redeemed there. Browning now could see the significance of the second view clearly in *Men and Women*, five years after his own religious crisis, and his thought on the Renaissance allowed him to incorporate his Christological perceptions into the aesthetic context. The two views of the place of the Incarnation form two poles of contrast in the poem, and take the form of two views of life. One view understands man as held down by the body and only able to live fully when he has shed the outward vesture of decay, while the other sees man as composed of mortal body and immortal soul, both of which have needs to be satisfied and developed. The second view, which Browning believes was held by Fra Lippo Lippi, gives a proper stress to the assumption of humanity in the Incarnation without losing sight of the supernatural vocation of man. The rest of the poem begins to move about these poles of contrast.[9]

We can expect a new stress on love in these poems on art from *Men and Women*, and in *Fra Lippo Lippi* Browning has integrated the love symbolism so that it becomes a major structural device. The popular street song, based on the fruit and flower symbol for love and sensual pleasures, recurs throughout the poem, but always in different ways and at significant points in the thought. It underlines or contrasts with what

[9]The two poles might be called the "this-worldly" and the "other-worldly." The former has a group of symbols and themes which are divided into those connected with business (especially the Medici family and their patronage), and those connected with love (with the symbols of fruit and flowers). The other-worldly also divides neatly into two: those symbols associated with the Prior and his thought (the desire for as nearly pure spirit as possible—just enough body to carry the soul), and on the other hand the ideals of a sort of monastic comfort in this life (the bread, grapes with their eucharistic symbolism, the fat monk, habit, girdle, and so on).

has gone before and what comes after the song, thus fulfilling its symbolic role of love in the critical moment acting to crystallize an epiphany. The flower imagery is also often connected with death imagery (the Incarnation, Good Friday, and the Resurrection, again the pattern of *Christmas-Eve and Easter-Day*) so that in the street song there is a combination of the two worlds of experience, the this-worldly and the other-worldly:

> *Flower o' the broom*
> *Take away love, and our earth is a tomb!* (53-4)

> *Flower o' the peach,*
> *Death for us all, and his own life for each!* (248-9)

The Christian connotations are not obscure. The flower symbolism used in the painting of the Madonna refers to perfection, as the culmination of the monologue issues in the synthesis of two areas of symbol and poles of contrast. The "Madonna and her babe" are painted with a "bowery flowery angel-brook, lilies and vestments," the union of body and soul symbols, of this- and other-worldly to deny the exclusive emphasis on soul. The Madonna-and-child representation of the Incarnation gathers together the different views on art, the place of the individual (the Prior's niece as St. Lucy),[10] and the religious and psychological symbolism as it shows the coming of the divine into the human sphere of experience. Man's place, the artist's place, is now of central importance in a divinely ordered, natural creation. The new freedom of the Renaissance presents man as the centre of the picture, living in *this* world, and working out his salvation in it.[11] Browning sees

---

[10]The prior's niece, an ordinary, identifiable person, has become St. Lucy—and this ties in neatly with the beginning of the poem where the men of the watch were picked out to serve as models for the artist to use. We may wonder if the Prior's niece is really his mistress so that a level of rather bitter irony comes from his remarks on the flesh. The habit was well known to Browning, as witness "cousin" in *Andrea del Sarto*, or "nephew" in *The Bishop Orders His Tomb*. Perhaps the niece is really the Prior's daughter. Or could this use represent love as an earthly passion transformed at the end of the poem into the aspirations of the soul for the divine love in the company of saints?

[11]Typical of the new approach were Cimabue (1240?-1302?), the teacher of Giotto, and Massaccio (1401-1428?), whom Browning understandably called the pupil of Fra Lippo although he was actually his mentor. Browning had used Cimabue earlier as a type of the new artist in his reference to the renaming of the street in *Pictor Ignotus* (DeVane, *Handbook*, 156). He had also used, DeVane tells us (*Handbook*, 217), Filippo Baldinucci's *Delle Notizie de' Professori del Desegno da Cimabue. . . .* , and mentioned the artist in *Old Pictures in Florence*. Browning knew much at first hand as well as from his reading of the works of the Italian Renaissance about the development of Italian painting, and from his own collection of Italian masters.

the changes in climate as a motion towards spiritual and artistic freedom, summarized in a striving from darkness to light:

> . . . As one by a dark stair into a great light,
> Music and talking. (362–3)

The light and dark patternings of the monologue are subtly developed. At the beginning the torches are thrust into Fra Lippo's face and this action highlights the central figure in the dark. Then there is a general movement towards illumination, both internal and external, until at the end the artist cries, "No lights, no lights," but the "grey beginning" of the dawn has come—the dawn of another day, the sunrise of another and fresher age.[12]

Fra Lippo himself manipulates the time sequence of the poem as he talks from about midnight until dawn, but in the poem the time is foreshortened. Within this time he also includes another scheme, the time-sequence of his life. He talks for a while about the present, but then moves to reflect about childhood in graphic and ironic terms. Then the story moves towards the present, and the views of men and art become clearer, until he states his developed creed:

> I always see the garden and God there
> A-making man's wife: and, my lesson learned,

[12]Browning's estimate of the Italian artists at the beginning of the Renaissance is more accurate than it might seem at first glance. His judgment is backed up by the Curator of the Louvre, René Huyghe, who summarizes the situation: "Two schools, those of Sienna and Florence, led the movement [towards liberation]. At the end of the XIIIth century, the two great pioneers Cimabue and Duccio broke away from the traditional technique. They already outlined the opposition between the two schools; Florence more intellectual and spiritual, more absorbed in beautiful composition, and Sienna, more sensitive and spontaneous, seeking charm and the pleasures of the heart. . . . Giotto, the Florentine, gave the first complete page of Italian art in his frescoes of Assisi and Padua: the truth of form and expressive life, dominated by the discipline of spirit which organizes and harmonizes. For almost a century Florence was to live under his influence, along with Gaddi and Daddi. . . . Meanwhile Simone Martini unfolded the evolution of his art and that of Sienna, full of charm and grandeur and refined delicacy, tender, sensitive descriptiveness. . . . Florence evolved a more methodical and realistic science. Fra Angelico still preserved all the religious ardour of the Middle Ages in a serene, spiritual mood of elevation but included new preoccupations with matter and perspective. The rehonouring of antique sculpture taught the truth and beauty of the human form; from the ruins sprang a growing taste for architecture and harmonious composition. Masolino, and above all his pupil Massaccio, who died young, turned to classical art. . . . Fra Filippo Lippi epitomises this new art, realist in manner, profane in spirit, intellectual in method. He is the start of a less harsh, less tense and at times less pure form of painting." (*La Peinture Italienne: XIIIe-XVIIIe Siècle*, Paris, Les Editions Braun n.d., 2 volumes, I, 7–9).

Browning's poem has much of this critical spirit in it, and the light-on-the-dark-stairs symbol is admirable in catching up the revelatory effect of the artist's life and work.

> The value and significance of flesh,
> I can't unlearn ten minutes afterwards.
>
> (266–9)

Now he turns to the future which he foresees ("the morning-star's about to shine") and he questions the place of the artist in a period of conflicting idealogies. His conclusion is:

> This world's no blot for us,
> Nor blank; it means intensely, and means good:
> To find its meaning is my meat and drink.
>
> (313–15)

The opening of the poem presents a dramatic situation which, as the monologue progresses, becomes more and more complex. The conclusion of the poem involves a composite symbol; so that the psychological conflicts of the poem are resolved by it. In this resolution the dramatic situation is also wrapped up with a sense of finality; and yet the finality is also regarded as a beginning—the grey dawn. In the critical moment the poet tries to sum up an age as well as an individual, and a whole philosophy as well as a personal psychology. Fra Lippo has chosen wisely in the *kairos* that was presented to him, and he has redeemed the time by making use of the redemption that was wrought at an earlier *kairos*. Now he is living in a kind of redeemed time, an aesthetic kingdom which has analogical connections with the Messianic kingdom. In each, the event has occurred which redeemed the time, both spiritually and artistically, so in each there is a legitimate participation in a beginning as well as in a final end.

Browning regarded *Fra Lippo Lippi* very highly, not only as a fine monologue of the Renaissance, but above all because it stated, as clearly as could be done by means of the *persona*, Browning's own position in the literary climate in England as he challenged the established and accepted poetic theories. We know that Browning read the poem at a literary evening when Tennyson, Dante Gabriel Rossetti (who made his famous sketch of Tennyson that evening), and William Michael Rossetti were gathered with the Brownings. Tennyson read *Maud*, and Browning answered with his poem of that year (1855), *Fra Lippo Lippi*. DeVane comments that there was not "a better poem with which to challenge the orthodox conception of poetry in mid-nineteenth century, or one that better expresses the new elements in poetry which he was to introduce."[13] Browning must have seen Fra Lippo's place in art as very close to that which he occupied in poetry; the comparison is unflattering to neither. The occasion of examining the artistic situation in the Renaissance had, in the poet's mind, been given a contemporaneity so that he could see his vocation in the terms of Fra Lippo: to do, to know, and to love.

Browning put *Andrea del Sarto* in the place of honour in the second volume of his *Men and Women* and he gave the poem a meaningful sub-title, "Called 'The Faultless Painter.'" In *Andrea* as in *Fra Lippo* there are two poles of contrast about which the poem moves, and they are essentially the same poles, although called by different terms. In *Fra Lippo* we had to find a name for the poles ourselves, and we called them the "this-worldly" and the "other-worldly"; in *Andrea* Browning has provided the terms, the imperfect and the perfect, as exemplified (just as we saw in *Fra Lippo*) in Andrea's life and art. Browning chooses to make of the "Faultless Painter" the faulty husband; perfection in art is contrasted with moral failure. Instead of Fra Lippo's boisterous enthusiasm with all that he touches, Andrea is quiet and passive, content to live his rather unhappy life in the seclusion of Fiesole. Browning has chosen the evening hour of Andrea's life (just as significant a moment as the time chosen to portray Fra Lippo) when "a common greyness silvers everything," and with irony he concludes his thought, "All in a twilight, you and I alike." But Lucrezia is still able to have her lovers, and Andrea must wink at her behaviour. Lucrezia had caused him all of his trouble; for his mistake in marrying her, he must pay all his life. The moment of enthusiasm which first carried him off was not the true moment of insight. Andrea had not properly appreciated the time-with-content of the *kairos*. Opportunity had presented itself, and he had not the wisdom to assess it in the light of ultimate values. All of this background is caught up into the first lines of the poem when the quarrel is mentioned. Then we are presented with the reasons for it, with the reiterated stress on "to-morrow." There is a pathetic hope throughout the poem that the time which once was lost will be regained, and the life or love which remains will be redeemed. That hope accounts for the acute awareness of the passage of time in the poem—

---

[13]DeVane, *Handbook*, 218–19. Cf. DeVane, *Browning's Parleyings*, 170–3, 228–9; Orr, *Life and Letters of Robert Browning*, 203; [Hallam Lord Tennyson], *Alfred Lord Tennyson: A Memoir* (London: Macmillan, 1897), I, 390–1.

from "half-hour," "evening," "to-morrow," and "time lost." Through all of the changes of time Andrea perceives that his wife smiles, and it is not merely the smile of the model. She knows the irony in the dramatic situation and in her husband's words which he cannot see. She, after all, has her rendezvous.

Browning follows Andrea's pupil, Vasari (in his *Lives of the Painters*), in his interpretation of del Sarto. Vasari comments that Andrea would have been a much greater artist if he could have combined with his craftsmanship some of the fire of genius, the determination and strength of will, the passion and love, which so nobly characterized those artists who were less "perfect" but much greater than Andrea, artists like Michelangelo, Leonardo, or Raphael. From Vasari, then, as well as from his own thought about the place of absolutes in life (which had been rejected by him for many years), Browning derived the basis of his philosophy of the imperfect. Ruskin had popularized the doctrine in his essay "On the Nature of Gothic." From Mrs. Orr's *Life* we know that Browning knew John Ruskin by 1855,[14] and he must have known some of Ruskin's writings before that. Ruskin had forsaken the prevalent view of "art for art's sake" in favour of a doctrine more aptly called "art for life's sake," itself strikingly close to Browning's own view as formulated in the early poems and the *Essay on Shelley*. Ruskin held that the greatness of a work of art depended upon the grandeur and nobility of the ideas that informed it, rather than upon the technical perfection with which it was executed. So he wrote: "The greatest picture is that which conveys to the mind of the spectator the greatest number of the greatest ideas."[15] Art is conceived as a moral activity of man in which a whole realm of social ideas are also concurrent, and Browning agrees in his *Essay on Shelley* (1852), which he was writing while Ruskin was in the midst of his *Stones of Venice* (1851-3). The highest faculty in Shelley was his "simultaneous perception of Power and Love in the absolute, and of Beauty and Good in the concrete," and that faculty is very close to what Ruskin calls the "Theoretic Faculty," which stresses the moral perception of beauty by means of contemplation, and so reveals the Good Life. Art is not only an instru- ✓ ment for living more fully; it is a way to the Good Life. So Browning

[14]Orr, *Life*, 203, referring to the letter of Elizabeth Barrett Browning: "We account him [Ruskin] one among the valuable acquaintances made this year in England."
[15]*Modern Painters* (Orpington, Allen, 1888), IV, 379.

has been saying all along. The artist's task in creating the work of art is to raise the beholder to the point of vision too, as he had explained in *Sordello*; the nature of the artist's task in creation (analogous to God's work in creation) and his use of the mediate word (analogous to the Incarnation) leads to the plan of a totally re-oriented social organism (analogous to the Messianic kingdom).[16] Art is to have a moral effect on civilization in both Ruskin's and Browning's views. Poets are the unacknowledged legislators of the world, and must order their laws wisely. Perfection in law as in life or art means death. Once it is attained, there is no more moral striving for that which is unattained. When art strives and reaches perfection in technique, then there has to be a decline in creative power. Vigour turns into elaboration; design becomes ornamentation; beauty is replaced by the grotesque. So it is in morality, and so, Browning held, it is in religion. Karshish saw that Lazarus had perfect knowledge and so his life was already in effect ended. Doubt had been removed from his horizon to be replaced by certainty; he lived a passive death-in-life existence. Andrea is aware of the perfection he has attained in his own craft ("When I say, perfectly, I do not boast"), but he also knows that in the greater artists "there burns a truer light of God." He puts into words the philosophy of the imperfect, and it is his own condemnation:

> Ah, but a man's reach should exceed his grasp,
> Or what's a heaven for? All is silver-grey
> Placid and perfect with my art: the worse!
>
> (97-9)

Andrea had suffered a moral failure in his marriage (that is, a vital, crucial failure in respect to love) and in his experiences at the court of Francis (whether he really did make off with the money or not is of little consequence here; Browning thought so), and these failures were directly related to his failures in art. The gold that had been the cause of his failure with Francis is symbolized in the only gold that Andrea now possesses, the gold of Lucrezia's hair. Even this touch is ironic,

---

[16]The parallels between Browning's aesthetic theory and the use of the analogical system in modern writers on aesthetics is sometimes astonishing. Many illuminating correspondences exist between Browning and the thought of Jacques Maritain in his *Creative Intuition in Art and Poetry*, where he writes (50): "If it is true that art is a creative virtue of the intellect, which tends to engender in beauty, and that it catches hold, in the created world, of the secret workings of nature in order to produce its own work—a new creature—the consequence is that art continues in its own way the labour of divine creation. . . ."

because Andrea does not even possess that. His life is declined to the silver years, and his art is turned to the silver-grey. There is a constant progression towards death (seen even in the colour symbolism) which results from the grasping of the perfect. Even Lucrezia is perfect—her eyes, ears, brow, and mouth. But she has no mind. The perfect artist can paint the perfect model, and the result will be a faultless painting, but not even the pure craftmanship of Andrea can give to his wife the mind and soul which would create the truly great painting. Andrea has aspiration enough, but he has not the inspiration which can only come from the enjoyment of the moment of harmony, the moment of vision, the moment of love.[17] Before he can proceed to execute the inspired painting (as Fra Lippo could do), he has to be in contact with onto-logical reality in the form of love. He has to know "what Is" before he can come to "what Does." He has achieved perfectly according to his limited aim, but he is not of the very greatest rank of "poets." He can describe accurately (the first poet of Sordello's catalogue), as we know from his correction of the paintings of greater men, and he can see and portray the "whatness" of what he describes (the second rank of poets), but he is not a "Maker-see." He has not enough of Ruskin's seven "lamps" which illuminated the greatest art: Sacrifice, Truth, Power, Beauty, Life, Memory, and Obedience. We notice how many of these Browning has made the subject-matter, whether direct or indirect, of his own art, and he has related them to all the other interests of his own life.

Browning saw that perfection in art was as serious a defect as certainty in religion. Both tended towards sterility, and removed the meaning from life. Knowledge which is certain is one kind of perfection; it is completeness without the element of doubt. In art or life meaning is achieved by striving for the ideal which is itself unattainable in this life; but in a moment of vision (which is what Andrea lacked) the perspective is changed so that one sees far and with unusual clarity into the nature of the perfection which is beyond this life. One sees the implications of the Incarnation in their eternal aspect; in that light one

[17]Maritain puts the point like this in terms of aesthetic theory that agrees with Browning's teaching: "Because, in the last analysis, in art as in contemplation, intellectuality at its peak goes beyond concepts and discursive reason, and is achieved through a congeniality or connaturality with the object, which love alone can bring about. To produce in beauty the artist must be in love with beauty. Such undeviating love is a supra-artistic rule—a precondition, not sufficient as to the ways of making, yet necessary as to the vital animation of art—which is presupposed by all the rules of art." (*Creative Intuition*, 43–4)

sees the true relationship of things and people, because the moment of vision is in its way a perception of the ideal. Andrea failed where Fra Lippo succeeded, and the reason is not in the artist, but in the man who strives for the vision. Nobility of life and grandeur of vision are not guarantees of success in art and life, but they provide the suitable environment in which the eternal might appear in a blinding flash.[18]

Old Pictures in Florence has as its main symbol the Campanile of the Duomo in Florence, which was designed by Giotto and which is perhaps his greatest work. To Browning it is the ready-made symbol of the theory he was trying to express. The design of the Campanile is exquisite, and its execution is magnificent. However, the Campanile is still unfinished, and so it is imperfect. It stands reaching upwards for the perfection which is denied to it. It is the example of a personalized art, and is set by Browning against the impersonal Greek art. Michelangelo and Raphael have passed to the perfect life, thinks the poet as he looks at Florence, and their reward is that they "see God face to face." They have "all attained to be poets" hopes Browning in the echoes of the end of *Pauline* and the death of Aprile in *Paracelsus*. Browning refers to the highest kind of poets, the "Makers-see" of *Sordello*, and the attainment is like that of Paracelsus' own. Greek art, on the other hand, has expressed the quiddity, or perhaps just the external physical likeness of nature, without attaining to the real function of art.[19] Greek art is in its way perfect, and it is condemned:

> They are perfect—how else? they shall never change:
> We are faulty—why not? we have time in store. . . .
> 'T is a life-long toil till our lump be leaven—
> The better! What's come to perfection perishes.

[18]The blinding flash comes as the result of the creative intuition of the poet, holds Maritain: ". . . The creative intuition is an obscure grasping of his own Self and of things in a knowledge through union or through connaturality which is born in the spiritual unconscious, and which fructifies only in the work. So the germ . . . which is contained in the spiritual might of the free life of the intellect, tends from the very start to a kind of revelation—. . . to the humble revelation, virtually contained in a small lucid cloud of inescapable intuition, both of the Self of the poet and of some particular flash of reality in the God-made universe; a particular flash of reality bursting forth in its unforgettable individuality, but infinite in its meanings and echoing capacity." (*Creative Intuition*, 83, 84)

[19]Browning sees the Greek failure (especially in *Protus*) as a failure in individuality as well as in true poetic function. So says Maritain: "Greek art is entirely intent on Things. . . . Man, privileged as his figure may be, remains an object in Nature and a thing in the cosmos, subordinate to the perfection and divinity of the universality of Things. A certain individualism starts to assert itself, it is true, but only as to the artist's individual talent or mastery, not as to his individual self-interiority. . . . The inner mystery of personality was not yet revealed to man." (*Creative Intuition*, 19)

Things learned on earth, we shall practise in heaven:
Works done least rapidly, Art most cherishes.

(123–32)

Giotto's Campanile is the example of the work of art that is done slowly and is most cherished. It tells more in its incomplete state of man's aspirations, dreams, and visions than the completed tower could ever do. Giotto is a "Maker-see" because in his incomplete masterpiece he sets forth all of man's passions; man glories that such a work is contemplated and erected to its present grandeur, but he also grieves that it is not finished. In the analogy of creation, the incompletion of the work of art is like the presence of sin in the created universe. Man's destiny is to be higher than the angels' because he is called to share in the life of God himself by means of the Incarnation; just so, the work of art is in the highest order completed by the artistic imagination in the mind of the greatest artist who gives this vision of completion to his beholders or readers. Browning is still reworking earlier thoughts that he had expressed in the first poems. Giotto's Campanile can stand in the poem for "the golden hope of the world," with the motto " 'God and the people,' " just because Giotto's creative activity is analogous to God's, and his work only finds its meaning within the context of God's acts in creation and redemption. Giotto, Aprile, and Browning can all cry:

Stay; I know,
I know them: who should know them well as I?
White brows, lit up with glory; poets all! . . .
Yes; I see now. God is the perfect poet,
Who in his person acts his own creations.

(*Paracelsus*, II, 644–9)

The artists of the Renaissance gain the plaudits "for daring so much, before they well did it," as Browning again stresses the significance of the poetic visionary. Florence, under the rule of Austria, cannot cultivate the love of beauty and truth that are liberating in themselves. But Browning calls upon his prophetic powers and looks ahead to the time when Florence will be free, and the symbol of her freedom will be the golden Campanile. Browning, no less than Ruskin, has connected the life of art and the life of the free individual in the free state. Art is seen in this poem as a social force, expressing the desire for freedom, and the creative activity itself suggests the means of attaining civil liberty. The artists whom Browning praises have left their individual mark upon the history of painting, and each artist has been free to create what he wishes to express; so it must be in Florence. If she wishes to become free and creative again, she must assert her independence and her individuality.

Another of the poems in which Browning expounds the philosophy of the imperfect is *A Grammarian's Funeral*. Here Browning is not so much concerned with art as he had been in the other poems we have examined in this section, but with the basic disciplines at the root of the fine arts. The old scholar's disciples carry the body of the grammarian to his resting place, and the movement is symbolic of the rise of learning in Europe. The man had to sacrifice his life (and we remember that sacrifice is the first of Ruskin's seven "lamps") to his rather mechanical study of linguistics, which he cultivated to an art, if not a fine art. That study, he well knew, was the basis of further study of the classics, and upon it the development of the vernacular depended. "This man decided not to Live but Know—," says one of the pallbearers, and so he is to be buried where the meteors shoot, on the mountain-top, instead of in the city where people merely "live." The meaning of the grammarian's life was found in the fact that he could not know all that he wished to know. His knowledge was limited, but he stretched his intellectual powers as far as they would reach, knowing that death would end his struggle. His knowledge is what Maritain calls "poetic knowledge" because it is "fully expressed only in the work."[20] Here is the same pattern of movement in the monologue that we have seen in Browning's other poems. The movement is a quest, and the object is the place of fulfilment.[21] *A Grammarian's Funeral* is one more indication of the way that Browning was thinking about that period of crisis, the Renaissance, during his stay in Italy when he could himself effect the pattern of his poetry, his vocation, and his ideal. The monologue gives the lie to those who think that because Browning puts so much emphasis on love, he does so at the expense of knowledge and power. The grammarian desired to know as much as he could, and by desiring

[20]*Creative Intuition*, 86. Maritain continued in the same passage: "In the mind of the poet, poetic knowledge arises in an unconscious or preconscious manner, and emerges into consciousness in a sometimes almost imperceptible though imperative and irrefragable way, through an impact both emotional and intellectual or through an unpredictable experiential insight, which gives notice of its existence, but does not express it."

[21]Charles Graham Cotter, in "Chief Symbolic Patterns . . . in Robert Browning" (Ph.D. thesis, University of Toronto [1952]) argues that the quest of *Childe Roland* is thematic in Browning.

much he attained much. But that is not the exclusive judgment given on his life. The monologue has several objects, as have most of Browning's poems. It is an account of the funeral procession; it is the story of the grammarian's scholarly life; it shows his impact upon his disciples; it has something to say about philosophy and theology; it illustrates a pattern in Browning's own life and art. The symbolic procession is the march of the progress of a man as he attains to new intellectual heights, on the mountain-tops where the illuminating flashes occur. From the burial-place of the grammarian light will radiate to other minds: that is the real reason why he is buried on the mountain crest. His work of illumination is not finished; others will build upon the structure that he left, and the new structures will be the brighter for his labours. But despite his life of significant toil, even the knowledge which he sought was imperfect.

Browning has in these few poems set forth his ideas about painting. At the centre of it all is the knowledge that man's life is limited, but the limitations are always beyond his grasp. This is the root of the philosophy of the imperfect in Browning, because it is seen in the light of a perfect act, the revelation of God's love in the Incarnation. Man may err in two directions. He may ignore perfection altogether, and that leads to a corruption of the individuality and ultimately to death (as in *My Last Duchess* or *The Bishop*). Or man may attain the perfect in some limited way (as in *Andrea del Sarto*) where individuality is lost, and again death is the result. Real meaning comes through the creative intuition of the poet or artist (*Old Pictures in Florence*), the life of significant toil (*A Grammarian's Funeral*), or in doing, knowing, loving as much as possible (*Fra Lippo Lippi*).

The philosophy of the imperfect, deriving in Browning partly from his thought on the implications of the Incarnation for the painting of the Renaissance, is central to his concept of human personality, and his analysis of it in terms of power, knowledge, and love. The Renaissance monologues, no less than the theological ones, also bring out the very important aesthetic theories of Browning, especially linking the work of the poet and of God as creators. The poems on painting are particularly fruitful in showing the artistic side of the analogy of poetry and painting with the nature of God. Browning has learned with Augustine that "the Word is, in a way, the art of the almighty and wise God" (*De Trinitate*, VI.x.2). Maritain, who in his *Creative Intuition in Art and*

Poetry seems to echo many of Browning's aesthetic and theological ideas, makes the same point in almost the same terms:

It is in a theological form, and at the peak of the most abstract conceptualization, that the notions of person and personality were first explicitly offered to the human mind: namely, in the dogmatic formulas concerned with Christian faith in the divine Trinity—one Nature in three Persons—and in the Incarnation of the Word—a divine Person assuming human nature. . . . Western art passed from a sense of the human Self first grasped as object, and in the sacred exemplar of Christ's divine Self, to a sense of the human Self finally grasped as subject, or in the creative subjectivity of man himself, man the artist or the poet.[22]

This perception of selfhood on the part of the poet or artist is an ontological activity, and is basic to creative intuition in the highest order of poets (Browning's "Makers-see"). Our activity consists in a participation in that ontological activity so that we too can be meaningfully related to it:

What we receive . . . is an *intellectual gift*, a participation in the poetic knowledge and poetic intuition through which the poet has perceived a certain unique mystery in the mystery of the world; then, it is true, since poetic intuition is knowledge through emotion, we receive a participation in the poet's emotion—not in his feelings, I mean, but in his spiritualized and intentional emotion, in his emotion as *causing to see*. We receive a transient and incomparable knowing, a vision, a fleeting revelation.[23]

Put into technical aesthetic terms, that is substantially what Browning has been saying. His examination of the artistic function in painting was an examination of poetic knowledge, that is, creative intuition. Now, in the poems on music, he has to examine the transitory nature of the intuition.

2. THE MONOLOGUES ON MUSIC

The aesthetic experience of music provided Browning with opportunities of amplifying the thought on aesthetic theory that he had been

[22]Maritain, *Creative Intuition*, 20. Maritain's interpretation of Greek art, as we have seen, is similar to Browning's, and so is his analysis of the art of the Renaissance, which at first discloses the "more human depths" of the mystery of the Person of Christ who is at the centre of thought. Then the human self and human subjectivity is internalized, leading to the outburst of individualism—"a sudden beholding of the sublimity of the artist's calling and of the new power and ambition afforded to him by science, by anatomical knowledge, mathematics, perspective, and the discovery of three-dimensional representation in painting, which intoxicated with glory the great Italians" (*ibid.*, 21–2).

[23]*Ibid.*, 210. Maritain quotes C. E. M. Joad (*Matter, Life, and Value*, 396): "In the appreciation of music and pictures, we get a momentary and fleeting glimpse of the nature of that reality to a full knowledge of which the movement of life is progressing. For that moment, and so long as the

developing in his poems on painting. Browning was intrigued with the ontological differences between music and painting. He knew that paintings have to be looked at in specific locations, and may be totally seen in one whole visionary examination as the entire expanse of canvas is opened to the view. Music does not have this static quality, but rather is characterized by its discontinuous, fleeting, and linear existence. In that a painting has a total, simultaneous presence, it is a being; but music lacks that simultaneity, and in that it exists when it is being performed or heard, it is really more accurately put into the ontological category of becoming.[24] Painting and music *are* not in the same way. Browning saw that in his own poetry he was trying to do the same things on the ontological level that the musician was trying to do in music. Both use rhythm, colour, weight, design, no less than painting, but music and poetry, in contradistinction to painting, are linear. But painting has always tried to describe itself in terms of poetry or music, using the critical vocabulary associated with the other art.[25] Browning tried in his poems on music to explore some of the implications of this approach to the fine arts, always concerning himself with the centrality of the Incarnation as the supreme artistic event in the ordered universe. Time naturally moves into a position of greater importance in the music monologues than in the poems on painting, although Browning has retained the same historical perspective.

Browning dealt with music several times, in *A Toccata of Galuppi's*

glimpse persists, we realize in anticipation and almost, as it were, illicitly, the nature of the end. We are, if we may so put it, for a moment *there*. . . ."

[24]Étienne Gilson has recently written extensively on the ontological connection between painting and music in his Mellon Lectures in the Fine Arts, *Painting and Reality*, chapter I, "Physical Existence," in which he says: "In a first sense music exists, in the same way as poetry, under the form of conventionally acceptable signs, written or printed on sheets of paper and signifying, for those who know how to read them, certain sounds or combinations of sounds. These signs or musical symbols . . . enjoy a physical existence, but they are not music. Music has no other actual existence than that of the actually existing sounds, and because sounds exist only while they are being actually produced, music exists only, precisely qua music, while it is being actually performed. This entails the immediate consequence that music pieces have a discontinuous mode of existence." (30, 31; cf. also 34, 35, 47)

[25]Cf. Gilson, *Painting and Reality*, 63: "Painting then feels tempted to describe itself in terms of music. If the phenomenology of aesthetic existence were more advanced than it is, the interaction of our experience of paintings in time and of their substantial stability in space could be analysed with more precision than can now be done. Higher literary and art criticism has long held it lawful artistically to look for musical analogies in poetry, for poetic analogies in painting, and for pictorial analogies in both poetry and music. Artists and art critics do not need philosophers to realize that such lofty speculations are possible; it is, however, to be hoped that philosophy will someday discover the reasons why, in their own order, these speculations are not only legitimate, but sources of the highest among the joys accessible to understanding."

and *Master Hugues of Saxe-Gotha*, both printed in *Men and Women* (1855), and in *Abt Vogler* in *Dramatis Personae* (1864). The first two poems, like those on painting which appeared in *Men and Women*, are probably referred to by Browning in his letter to Milsand from Florence on February 24, 1853: "We live wholly alone here. I have not left the house one evening since our return. I am writing—a first step towards popularity for me—lyrics with more music and painting than before, so as to get people to see and hear. . . ."[26] Browning is not speaking of mere didacticism in poetry; he has a higher goal which is nothing short of teaching the Good Life. By means of the poems on painting and music he is striving to become his own ideal of the highest kind of poet, the one who imparts "the gift of seeing to the rest." He wants people to "see" and "hear" painting and music by means of his poetry, and underneath them to see and hear the meaning of the divine life that pulsates through them both. He wishes to show the incarnational implications of painting and music through poetry, and thereby teach the sacramental nature of all life.

A Toccata of Galuppi's moves about two poles of contrast like the poems on painting. The speaker in the monologue muses about the conflicts between the coldness of Galuppi's formal music and the warmth and gaiety of the life of Venice where he wrote. The formality of the music strikes the monologuist as the perfection of death, leading to "dust and ashes," but there is a paradox. Actually it is Galuppi's music that has survived to the present, speaking in rather strange austere tones about a Venice that was quite different—familiar and happy. But the people who inhabited that Venice have all gone to their graves, while the music that perhaps should have suggested the *timor mortis* theme, reminding them of the triumph of death in its inevitability, has outlived them. Galuppi's music is enjoying a kind of eternal existence, outliving the composer, and yet being itself the means by which he may live on in a personal immortality to speak the same message over and over to future generations if they will hear it. Browning is not suggesting that there is nothing after this life, but rather that the meaning of this life comes from its nobility, its service, and its illumination by the divine life of God. Galuppi, by his art, is still able to call people to the higher life, to make people "see and hear," as Browning wrote to Milsand. Music itself is moving, patterned,

---

[26]Quoted in DeVane, *Handbook*, 207.

ordered, and to some extent timeless. It is contrasted with life, which is transient, disordered, and completely bound by time. The kind of life that is presented in the poem is the life of Venice, that is, the life of the world; it is itself fleeting and based on the senses. There seems to be love in the poem, but it is a shallow love, not the merging of the soul of the lover in the soul of the beloved that Browning demands. The teleological question that the music should suggest to the people of Venice, "Must we die?", is answered by them with a kind of futile hope, "Life might last! we can but try!" and so they go on to more love-making, satisfying temporal ends. The ironic words when the music stops for a moment are revealing because they show that the patron of culture has little idea of what was being played (and even less of its implications) while he sported. He utters a blanket statement to cover any eventualities, pretending that he was talking when he was love-making:

> "Brave Galuppi! that was music! good alike at grave and gay!
> I can always leave off talking when I hear a master play!"
>
> (26–7)

This "lover" does not realize that to appreciate music as art requires attention and above all silence. The empty air is, in a sense, analogous to the painter who has to have his blank canvas or the poet his blank page before he starts to create. All of this is analogous to the act of God in creating the universe out of nothing.[27] When the lover talked through the music, the aesthetic moment was lost, and with it the meaning of life. Then death took the listeners, the ones who had "never seen the sun" of illuminated life, the joy in art, in doing, in being, and in deep love. Galuppi had given to himself a kind of immortality in his music because he poured into his music something of his soul. The speaker asks, "What of soul was left, I wonder, when the kissing had to stop?" Here there are several levels of meaning. The people of Venice who wasted their lives did not prepare for their deaths by living deeply and nobly. The kissing stopped when the music was interrupted, and there had been no moment of vision between the so-called lovers. No souls were given in love; no union was possible, and so there is a mockery of love. Furthermore, the kissing is stopped by death. When the true

[27] See Gilson, *Painting and Reality*, chapter IV, "The Ontology of Paintings," and especially section 2, "Nothingness and Creation."

music of life stops (which the Venetians did not choose to hear, just as they did not hear Galuppi's music), then what of the soul is left when it has not been nurtured in life? The gold of the women's hair flowed down over their bosoms, where there should have been a greater and more permanent gold, the gold of love in the living heart's soul. But it was not used; life was not lived, and all has come to dust and ashes, while the music of Galuppi points its rather bitter moral.

Music, then, is like painting. It is an ordered and careful art, and that points for Browning to an ordered and careful life. Music says something important about man's condition, just as painting did; it is perhaps better equipped by the nature of its being to say more about the fleetingness of life, about the moment of artistic creation, and about the ephemeral quality of love's true intuition. But by means of music a new world could be opened to those who hear, just as painting opens one for those who see. The artist's task is to make people see and hear the new relationships within life which the art shows, so that the moment of musical or artistic ecstasy can be treasured as something perpetually illuminating in the memory. The light of the moment of apperception gives a new meaning to all that comes after it. It is a kind of distillation of beauty into colour or sound; it is a fitting of the infinite to the finite; it is an analogue to Incarnation. But the aesthetic experience must be appreciated by willing ears and ready eyes, by an act of choice, and it is not to be ignored as the Venetian lovers did. Then only can it be recollected from memory's ear and eye and give meaning to life. St. Augustine discussed the problem in his treatise *De Trinitate*, considering the powers of the mind as the image of the Trinity:

Again, if one were to apprehend the ordered rhythm of certain transient artistic and musical sounds extending over a period of time, that tune, though resting without time in some secret and profound silence, can still be as long as it can be heard by the mind. Yet what the glance of the mind, transient though it was, caught from it and stored in the memory, after so to speak gulping it down, this it will be able to ponder in some measure by recollection, and transfer what it thus learned into a systematic shape.[28]

The activity of the mind in recollection and giving of systematic shape to what memory cherishes is the exercise from which the next artistic

[28]*De Trinitate*, XII, xiv, 22–3; cf. also *Confessions*, XI, xxvii, 34–xxviii, 38; and Gilson, *Painting and Reality*, chapter I, section 2. Similar methods are applied to the poetic use of music in words by Maritain in *Creative Intuition*, chapter VIII, "The Internalization of Music."

creation is made in the new poetic activity of any art. The illuminating experience is cherished in the memory to illuminate other experiences. That is how Galuppi's music is to work for those who hear; that is how the Incarnation is to illuminate the totality of life. And through all of Browning's poem chimes the paradoxical chord, *Vita brevis, ars longa.*

Master Hugues of Saxe-Gotha is much more reluctant than Galuppi to tell what his music means, or rather to allow it to be discovered. Nor does the earnest questioning of the musing organist prevail when he asks, "What do you mean by your mountainous fugues?" In effect this means: "What does your life mean? What does it all add up to? What is its value?" Hugues' spectral visage, peeping from among the organ pipes says that the organist has the mere notes under control, but he has not the soul of the music, that which led Hugues to be called "Master." The organist is moving the succession of musical notes in the prescribed pattern, but he is not yet weaving the mysterious incantation which speaks of Hugues' genius. He is merely interpreting Hugues, but in doing that he wishes that he could have some certain knowledge about Hugues' permanent value. Browning is here engaged in a most difficult philosophical problem in metaphysics. He wonders why the artist who is performing the music cannot get back to the original genius which is supposed to have inspired the composition in the first instance. The problem involves the mode of existence of music, that it is discontinuous, and does not ever exist in what could be regarded as a permanent and ideal form. Each composition is open to new interpretation which may reveal hidden depths even though they could not be interpreted by the composer himself. Painting exists in a different way, so that it may be grasped totally as the artist informed and completed it.[29] The painter can communicate his inspiration directly; the musician depends upon the virtuoso interpreter, and so music becomes the more mediate of the arts. This is the connection that Browning needs to find for the relation between music and the Incarnation. Poetry is akin to music in that both depend upon the mediate sound for the communication of thought and emotion; the Incarnation depends upon the mediate Word for the communication of the gospel of salvation. The Word comes in its *kairos*, or appointed time, and then it is received. Just so the poetic word comes in a time-situation, a linear

[29]See Gilson, *Painting and Reality*, chapter III, "Duration," section 3, "Life and Death of Paintings."

structure, and a historical context in which it is to be set and assimilated. And in music there is a *kairos* too, a time not only of measured bars, but also a time-with-content. That is precisely the problem of the musician in *Master Hugues*. He is aware of the music as it is on the page, and he knows the historic context, but he is not certain about the content involved in the *kairos* to make it revelatory. Hugues has not provided in his music, as Galuppi had done, his soul which speaks to the soul of the performer or hearer. He has not lived deeply enough to incorporate into his music something of the feelings that make life worth while, the stuff from which Maritain's "creative intuition" is able to spring.

Soul in the music is unperceived not because of the performer's lack of attention, because the music is closely analysed as it is being played, and the parts of the fugue are laid out before us, as Browning uses a clever device. Each of the five voices of the fugue acts as though it were a separate person, and all are engaged in a furious musical conversation which ranges from quietness to argument and back again. The poem moves on towards climax and the organist feels that there is something being said which is significant, "if one but caught the import." But the gold of the meaning, symbolically represented in the gilt of the baroque church, is concealed by the very striving of the music as the fugal statements wrestle and surge to and fro, so well represented by the intricacies of the spider's web. The player asks if Master Hugues' meaning is that life is just such a mass of weavings as his music portrays, or as the spider exhibits in his craft, while God's truth is clouded over by the shroud of death and ignorance that man weaves for himself:

> So we o'ershroud stars and roses,
>   Cherub and trophy and garland;
> Nothings grow something which quietly closes
>   Heaven's earnest eye: not a glimpse of the far land
> Gets through our comments and glozes.
>
> (116–20)

Browning brings his usual and favourite symbols into play in making the wider connotations of the poem reach out to the connections with the rest of his poetry. We find the use of gold (= truth) that we saw in *Andrea* and *Fra Lippo*, the star (= inspiration, as in *My Star*), roses (= love, as in *Women and Roses*), and the same expected trinity of symbols, the cherub (= love), the trophy (= power), and the garland

(= knowledge) which are clouded over in the poem so that man does not catch sight of the glory. Hugues left "a mere mountain in labour," unlike the grammarian, whose life was one of *significant* toil. That is the fact that the organist is so reluctant to accept—that all of the labour of Master Hugues has been expended on insignificant mountains. In a sudden burst the musician plays some Palestrina, thinking that the gold in the roof, the gold of truth will then be seen, but the symbolic candle gutters, and all is dark. Hugues is still a mystery. He had developed the art of the fugue to such a high degree that it ceased to move as music and became something closer to mathematics. He had attained a kind of mechanical perfection, and had lost his individuality which would have redeemed his art so that the musing musician could have caught a clear sight of Hugues and his meaning. The formalism of the fugue speaks of an historic period of imitation in the eighteenth century. Browning thought that the pure art of Italy (as represented in the candle) had declined almost to oblivion. Galuppi's toccata had a notable effect upon the meditation of its player, but Hugues' fugue leads only to frustration. Art must have an impact on life so that it appears in a new perspective; it must enable men to see more clearly and deeply and widely than before. Hugues had not sufficiently grasped the life-enhancing ecstasy that comes from the aesthetic moment, and so he could not write it into his music. His failure was a personal one, and so his own individuality is lost to the modern interpreter who cannot understand his music. But the failure is also one of the historical period, the eighteenth century, for which Browning had little sympathy. It was not an age of crisis, and the implications of the meaningful events in the life of civilization, in art (humanism), and in theology (the Incarnation), lost their bearing on life. The result was that life lost its meaning. There was time aplenty, in the sense of *chronos*, but the *kairos* was sacrificed to a delight in the insignificant. Browning has not yet presented his fully developed thought on the place of music among the fine arts. He needed the nine years of meditation from *Men and Women* (1855) to *Dramatis Personae* (1864) with his thought on poetry, painting, love, and religion, before he could pursue the theme again.

Abt Vogler is the most finished and skilful of Browning's poems upon music, and it will stand beside any of his works for depth of thought and eloquence of expression. Abt Vogler was, DeVane tells us,[30] the

[30]*Handbook*, 290–2.

originator of the musical system in which Browning was trained by his master, John Relfe. But it is more important for the study of Browning to learn that Vogler was a man who was little known in his own time, a pious man, and a brilliant extemporizer, thus combining the qualities that Browning wished to study: the reticent artist who is jealous of preserving his own life and individuality, especially in respect to religion, and yet who is most revealingly seen in the moment of artistic activity itself. Unlike either Galuppi or Master Hugues, Vogler is himself the performer and the speaker of the monologue. Browning has avoided the difficulties of a separate monologuist which interfered with the appreciation of the kernel of the music's meaning in the other two poems. By combining the roles of monologuist and musician, Browning achieves an added intensity of effect as poetry and music become mutually illuminating. Furthermore, Browning has removed the mediator of the musical experience by going directly to the source, the abbé actually engaged in the exercise of his art of extemporizing. Vogler is not only speaking about what he knows, and playing the music as well; he is meditating in music upon the instrument that he has invented. The creative artist is given superb poetry to express profound thought by playing on the instrument of an inventive craftsman. Browning is bringing together the craftsmanship of Master Hugues (to some extent parallel to the perfection of Andrea), and the philosophic thought of Galuppi (like the thought of Fra Lippo Lippi), into the new *persona* about whom Browning weaves many of his most characteristic themes.

Abt Vogler begins by seeing as a whole the music that he has been creating by the process of extemporization or improvisation. He is engaged in a most difficult metaphysical activity, that of seeing as a unified whole what is by nature partial and linear. His activity is essentially mystical in that it is analogous to what the religious mystic is doing when he attempts union with the wholeness of God whom the theologians supremely describe by the term "pure act." [31] Abt Vogler

[31]See Gilson, *Painting and Reality*, chapter IV, section 2, "Nothingness and Creation," 126–7; and chapter IX, "The Significance of Modern Painting" (270–1) in which he writes: ". . . If one can speak of God as of the supreme Artist, his art is certainly innocent of any groping and of any becoming due to what would be for him the incomplete previsibility of his own works. . . . According to Christian theology, creative power belongs to God alone, and the world of creatures owns no parcel of it. But it does not take a divine power to achieve novelty in the communication of existence and in the forming of man-made beings. This is what artists do. . . . Painters are the makers of new visual forms whose proper function is to make intelligibility perceptible to human

is attempting to see the "static being" of his art in a way that is appropriate to painting when he is really dealing with an art which is more accurately described as a "moving becoming." Browning is trying to place Vogler in a metaphysical universe where it is possible to perceive the wholeness of a work of art, not as in painting, at the end of the more or less creative activity when the inspiration has been fully digested, but in the actual moment of creative intuition. The situation is paradoxical, because Vogler is combining the arts of painting (his picturing of the musical structure), music (the fabric of which the structure is made, and the real substance of the meditation), and poetry (the medium through which the aesthetic experience is to be communicated):

> For think, had I painted the whole,
> Why, there it had stood, to see, nor the process so wonder-worth:
> Had I written the same, made verse—still, effect proceeds from cause,
> Ye know why the forms are fair, ye hear how the tale is told;
> It is all triumphant art, but art in obedience to laws,
> Painter and poet are proud in the artist-list enrolled:—
> But here is the finger of God. . . .
>
> (43–9)

Browning gives to music an ontological reality which it does not have in ordinary musical compositions (in that we cannot speak of *the* Kreutzer Sonata as though it were a self-existent reality independent of the performer or the hearer or the manuscript). The ontological reality which he has cleverly chosen comes into being in its ideal form as an extemporization, and there exists in both its ideal and in its realized form: it is complete as it springs in a moment of intuitive insight from the composer and as soon as it is realized, it also perishes:

> But here is the finger of God, a flash of the will that can,
> Existent behind all laws, that made them and, lo, they are!
> And I know not if, save in this, such gift be allowed to man,
> That out of three sounds he frame, not a fourth sound but a star.
>
> (49–52)

---

sight. . . . In a created universe whatever exists is religious because it imitates God in its operations as well as in its being. If what precedes is true, art, too, is religious in its very essence, because to be creative is to imitate, in a finite and analogical way, the divine prerogative, exclusively reserved for HE WHO IS, of making things to be."

Cf. also Bernard Berenson, *Aesthetics and History*, I, "Value," section "The Aesthetic Moment," 93; and II, "Illustration," section "What Visual Art Can Do," 102.

The extemporizing does not have permanence but the brevity of its mere temporal existence is a glimpse of eternity. Vogler and Browning are right in regarding the spontaneous creation as a structure, even as a palace of art, and each of the notes contributes its special quality to the whole. The voices of the fugue which Master Hugues composed, a highly technical and organized piece of music, seemed to speak in argument and conflict. But the extemporizing of Vogler is harmonious, each element in the fabric of the composition contributing to the total effect. The palace of music is compared with the construction of Solomon's palace, which took thirteen years. Vogler wishes that his creation could linger in existence like the creation of Solomon, but his artifact is created simply to fade and die, only to be replaced by another, perhaps inferior, perhaps more beautiful by far. The musical extemporization, then, is analogous to life: it is short, fading, and quickly comes to death, remaining in the memory of those who can still recall it. But the music also tells of the meaning of life, as it can be lifted into a mirror of the eternal life of heaven. Vogler's art tells of his aspirations as he reached for the music of heaven, but it also tells of his limitations. The passions of the composer had enabled him to lift earth and all that it could afford up as high as possible, but he still needed the spark from heaven which would transform earth. At the moment when his inspiration seemed to be complete and he became the mere medium for the musical expression, then "earth had attained to heaven, there was no more near nor far." That moment is the moment of revelation when heaven and earth are joined, as in the Incarnation. It is the moment out of time and space ("no more near nor far"), two conditions needed for the appreciation of the static art like painting; but here they have been abolished. The moment is the springing of eternity *in* time, and yet beyond it, because it transcends it. The moment gave meaning to all of the music that Vogler had composed before, and so to all of the life that had gone before. As for the future, the structure of the music looks ahead to that, and sees part of the perfection that will then be. As for the present, it is redeemed, and the artist is redeemed in the process, because he has glimpsed a vision of the perfection of heaven. He has not the certainty of Lazarus who lives wholly in the light of the other world, but he has seen enough to transform his attitude to reality in this world.

Now, in the moment of attainment, the musician can contemplate

with extraordinary brilliance the thing that he has wrought. He has
emptied his soul into his music, and now he compares the achievement
to the expression of the soul in another medium. This is the natural
course that Browning's thought would follow, since it is his custom
constantly to relate the modes of communication possessed by the
different arts. If Vogler had painted, the process would not have been
so "wonder-worth," so filled with the sheer inspiration of the moment
which transformed the notes into beauty. If he had written down the
emotions which he had experienced, then that would have taken too
much time (as would painting) and he also would be bound by a more
strictly linear art. Browning saw the difficulties of expressing in the
constrictions of the written line the simultaneous effect of the illuminative moment, and he had discussed the problem as far back as
Sordello. The music of improvisation allowed one to hear the art, and
to have the pattern revealed almost in a flash, and just as suddenly the
whole pattern is gone forever:

> Well, it is gone at last, the palace of music I reared;
>   Gone! and the good tears start, the praises that come too slow;
> For one is assured at first, one scarce can say that he feared,
>   That he even gave it a thought, the gone thing was to go.
> Never to be again!   (57–61)

Painting permitted one to see the effect of the moment of inspiration
as it was carefully modelled into the finished combination of colours
and forms; it could be grasped in a moment, but the original inspiration
was really further from one's grasp than in spontaneous music because
it was worked on by the craftsmanship which remembered the inspiration without continually experiencing it. In literature the process is still
more removed from the original impetus. The lines themselves have to
be read in a time- and space-sequence, and the impact of the spontaneous effect is lost simply by the time that passes in the reading of the
work of art. Vogler says that the art of the painter and the poet is "art
in obedience to laws." His own art is spontaneous creation where
intuition is given full reign. His act is perfectly free too, limited only by
the restrictions of his instrument or his visionary inspiration. Here again
there are important analogies with the free, spontaneous, and unlimited
act of God in Incarnation. Vogler is aware of the implications of his
thoughts and art as he calls inspiration "the finger of God," remember-
ing God's act in creation, as immortalized in Michelangelo's Sistine

fresco showing God's finger touching man's as he is created. This inspiration of the finger of God, or the Spirit of God, created the worlds, and still creates through the artist who can use the technicalities of music ("three sounds") to set forth the ideal perfection that he has seen ("a star").

The musician stops playing, and the palace of his art vanishes; the vision of the ideal is gone. Perfection is gone. It cannot constantly be experienced (as Lazarus possessed certainty, or Andrea perfection), but must be replaced, argues Vogler, with the definite act of mind, the willing choice which holds on to the memory of perfection once experienced. The choice is also made to hold on to the self that was the medium of the experience (the redemption of humanity and individuality, as in the Incarnation when human individuality received the stamp of its true value since it was itself the medium of the experience of revelation). The artist also chooses to cherish the love that brought it to be (analogous to the love of God in the Incarnation), and the love of God who is himself that love.

The extemporizer

> . . . must be saved because I cling with my mind
> To the same, same self, same love, same God: ay what was, shall be.
>
> (63–4)

By a very careful manipulation of the threads of the poem, Browning has once more brought us back to consider the "ineffable Name" that he had first introduced as a minor theme in connection with Solomon. At this point in the poem, there is a significant change in direction. Until now Vogler has been extemporizing upon his instrument, and meditating, almost rhapsodizing, upon the art of music. Then stanza VIII provides the bridge as the ultimate direction of his thoughts comes to him. In stanza IX Vogler turns to address "the ineffable Name" directly as the ground of art (the Inspirer of the palace which Vogler had made) and of life (the Creator of our bodies, and the heavenly dwelling, "houses not made with hands," for our souls). Vogler has seen the ontological ground of the being of art in the being of God:

> Doubt that thy power can fill the heart that thy power expands?
> There shall never be one lost good! What was, shall live as before;
> The evil is null, is naught, is silence implying sound;
> What was good shall be good, with, for evil, so much good more;
> On earth the broken arcs; in the heaven a perfect round.
>
> (68–72)

This has been the end of all of Browning's thought upon art and the aesthetic process, and it is characteristic of the man whom we saw moving in this direction in the monologues after *Christmas-Eve and Easter-Day* that he should come to a metaphysical and religious solution. Power is seen to be the expression of the controlled will of God, and it works for good both in the acts of God and in the analogous acts of the artist in using the power of expression which he has been given. Even evil, says Browning in a typical idea, is useful for good ("silence implying sound"). Earth is the broken arc of heaven, broken by the evil and ignorance and imperfection, but a true arc, nevertheless. What is imperfect and incomplete here is perfect and whole there:

> All we have willed or hoped or dreamed of good shall exist;
> Not its semblance, but itself; no beauty, nor good, nor power
> Whose voice has gone forth, but each survives for the melodist
> When eternity affirms the conception of an hour.
>
> (73–6)

In eternity is the *eskaton* of time which has already been fulfilled by the Incarnation; the good will be shown as it is in its reality; and the momentary conception of the composer will be shown to be the earnest of eternity. Failure and imperfection here will more clearly show the perfection and completion of heaven in "the fulness of the days." Here is Browning's more developed attitude to the first writings on the philosophy of the imperfect in the poems on art. He has progressed considerably in depth, and his answer is wholly religious. This is the ground for what some have too glibly called Browning's easy optimism. It is a religious attitude which is hard won through personal and artistic difficulties, and even this position is one which he thinks it is wise to question from time to time, as he does until the end of his days.

Meanwhile, for Vogler the life of honest doubt (as for Browning) is the right life. Sorrow is real, but it is also transient. Yet to a few men, to those who can see deeper and to whom more is revealed (because the action of God's revelation must be met in each person by the responsibility of man's response), to the bard, the seer, the prophet, the saint, the lover, the painter, and the poet, to each God whispers something of his truth in a visionary moment of inspiration. This truth is "known" by the musician as the type of the creative artist. The last stanza of the poem has moved back from the mountains of imaginative thought (like those in *A Grammarian's Funeral*) to the common life in the world among men. The musician strikes the common chord, and yet he is upon alien ground. Just so is earth alien to the man who has his citizenship in the heaven which he has glimpsed. The importance of Abt Vogler's life is that he "dared" and to some extent succeeded. But his reach still exceeded his grasp, and that is as it should be. He has not reached out within his own limitations like Andrea del Sarto, nor was he content to live in the world of the vision like Lazarus. He came back to fulfil the true poetic function that Browning had set up in his *Essay on Shelley* (to connect the two worlds of reality) and explained in *Sordello* (to make people see this connection). Vogler found the "C Major of this life," the centre of the keyboard, and so symbolically the true centre of life, related to all of the rest, and the centre in which all of the rest have their meaning. But the centre is primary, by which the accuracy of all the other notes is to be judged. So it is with the Incarnation, which stands in the centre of time like the middle C. It is also the connection between the two worlds of reality, and it so combines them in the person of Christ that they are really one. It is the task of theologians to explain this connection; it is the task of artists to illuminate the connection by examining man's highest creative activity. That is how Browning is fitting his poems on art and religion together, and that is the relation that he sees between poetry, painting, and music.

Browning has dealt with two of the three qualities or faculties of the three souls that he outlines in *A Death in the Desert*—doing and knowing. Meaning for life comes from the action of the will in striving for an unattainable goal, and knowing that the goal is still beyond reach. The art and the music of the Renaissance provided the material for this investigation. Browning has considered religious love, the other and greatest of the souls ("what Is"), but we have yet to examine his treatment of the love of the sexes and fit that into his total pattern.

PHYSICAL UNITY:
POETRY AND LOVE

> ... Ah, Sweet—
> The moment eternal—just that and no more—
> When ecstasy's utmost we clutch at the core
> While cheeks burn, arms open, eyes shut and lips meet!
>   (*Now*)

IN THE RELIGIOUS poems the Incarnation is the central religious doctrine for Browning. The Incarnation is to him the moment of God's supreme self-revelation, and it is the archetype of all other kinds of revelation. Thus poetic inspiration is grounded in the truth of the revelation of God, and for Browning both are equally real. The poet is a man who has a sacred function in carefully passing on to his generation and to posterity the inspiration that was given to him. He is expressing what Austin Farrer calls "the texture of human existence or the predicament of man,"[1] and he may relate this to the revelation of God; however, he does not do what the prophet exclusively does in speaking directly to people the message of God's mediate Word. The poet's images move under no less an active incantation than the prophet's, but the prophet's are constrained by the self-fulfilling will of God, rather than the creative imagination which is inspired by God in the poet. The poet is to use the three "souls" that Browning explained in *A Death in the Desert*, his poetic power, his knowledge, and his love for man, in interpreting and communicating his inspiration. In painting also, inspiration comes in a great flash to illuminate suddenly the work of the

[1]*The Glass of Vision*, 117.

artist. The painter, no less than the poet or the saint or the prophet must be consecrated to his art. All have their roles in history to make life more beautiful, and that is to make it more truly exist at its highest point.[2] That is how Browning saw the history of the arts: a movement towards the truth of reality in the Good Life. Music, while not providing as clear a pattern of history as painting, simply because of its discontinuous mode of being, is a more valuable means of examining the moment of inspiration itself. But there is one more area of human experience which was of primary concern to Browning in the poetry of his middle years, the poems which are related to the love of the sexes.

The Last Ride Together, first published in *Men and Women* (1855), provides a reader with a link between the poems on love and those on art. It is an attempt to analyse the various contributions which poetry, sculpture, and music can offer to life. The speaker, a rejected lover, concludes that love, even though it had been rejected, is more meaningful for life than any of the arts. He desires to go on a last ride with his beloved and again we have the favourite Browning device of the journey or quest, as always in Browning analogous to the archetypal journey of the Magi, kings themselves in their own countries, guided by the symbolic star to the place of revelation where the eternal is made temporal, and the temporal eternal in the act of God's love. So the speaker is trying to catch something eternal that he will be able to cherish in his memory during the temporal life that remains without his beloved. He chooses to search for it away from the world of men, on a last wild gallop:

> I and my mistress, side by side
> Shall be together, breathe and ride,
> So, one day more I am deified.
>   Who knows but the world may end to-night?

The last line is ironic, because in a real sense his world will end to-night when he is left to face life alone. He has glimpsed the teleological implications of the termination of his love, and so he must cherish all that he can of this last critical moment in the ride. The ending of his love occurs at a critical moment (since "the world may end to-night"), but the same critical moment is constantly present if one were only to think of it. Eternity is constantly trying to rush in upon the creative moment, but man will not let it take up its place to illuminate the past and future.

[2]Gilson, *Painting and Reality*, 271.

So it is with the lover in the poem. He realizes now that part of him is to die, but he wishes to keep what remains alive still oriented to this moment when it has known its greatest reality, when it most supremely knows what it is to be. The two figures seem ready to move along between heaven and earth, as nature endows the beloved with its beauty:

> Till flesh must fade for heaven was here!—
> Thus leant she and lingered—joy and fear!
> Thus lay she a moment on my breast.

"Then we began to ride." The speaker muses on the past—what it might have been if he had acted otherwise, and had other men's gifts. But the poet's verse cannot compare with the sheer joy in life that the ride gives, nor can the accomplishments of the sculptor or musician capture the sensation of striving action in the ride. The speaker realizes that, despite his moment of bliss, he "must lead some life beyond, have a bliss to die with." It is in this moment that he lives, but because he has not surrendered wholly to the inspiration, the moment is not as complete as it should be, as it is for the speaker in *In a Gondola*: "I have lived indeed, and so—(yet one more kiss)—can die!" The rejected lover has hunted for the "glory-garland" to place around his soul, but wonders if earth is so good, would heaven seem best. Heaven is come to him in his moment, and he yearns for an eternity that would prolong the moment of the ride, if he could capture that perfection:

> What if we still ride on, we two,
> With life forever old yet new,
> Changed not in kind but in degree,
> The instant made eternity,—
> And heaven just prove that I and she
> Ride, ride together, forever ride?

But this is illusion, mere idle dreaming, and it is not to be. The moment when he could have had his revelation fades and soon it is wholly gone. Life must still be lived, but it cannot be lived as though the chance for the moment had never been. It would have been possible for time and love and life to have been redeemed if the critical moment had been caught by the choosing act of will, but that was forfeited for musing on what might have been. The critical moment judges the rejected lover, and he is left with his memories of the love he had had, of the moment he had approached, of the last ride together, of the wishful desire to prolong the ride into eternity, and of the knowledge that all has vanished. Love, like art and religion, can be redemptive if it is made incarnate in life's critical moment.

Browning chose the superb lyric, *Love Among the Ruins*, to stand first in the first volume of *Men and Women*. The position was an important one, and so Browning chose an important poem to head his collection. As in so many of the monologues, two sets of contrasts and parallels are built up, centring on the symbols of the city and the plain. The first half of the initial five stanzas is devoted to a description of the pastoral landscape—evening, sheep, grass, and the little turret. The landscape is strikingly different from that of the two poems which Browning wrote on the two days previously (January 1 and 2, 1852), *Childe Roland* and *Women and Roses*. Browning is using the typically idyllic symbolism of sylvan literature to point to a golden age, and for him that means not only the dawn of civilization in the Garden of Eden (so scarcely at all the Greek mythological golden age), but also the pastoral setting of the new golden age at the Incarnation. That is the significance of this symbolism in Browning's Christian and poetic cosmology. The second half of each of the first four stanzas describes an imaginary picture of the way the plain must have looked many centuries before when the ruins were a great city, bursting with power, wealth, and beauty. This is the Babylon of the world into which the pastoral message of hope will come. Then in the second half of the fifth stanza a transition is made. We learn that the speaker goes to meet "a girl with eager eyes and yellow hair" in a turret where the charioteers prepared to race. Now in the remaining two stanzas we begin with the city and conclude with the meeting in the ruins. The lovers rush into each others' arms and "extinguish sight and speech each on each." The experience of love ("Love is best") has far more ultimate value than the efforts of the city civilization to conquer the world ("centuries of folly . . . with their triumphs and their glories"). The art and power and learning of the past have crumbled into ruins, but the ruins are made to serve the present moment by sheltering the love that two people cherish. In the process of history, *chronos* had swallowed the grandeur of Greece, the glory of Rome, but the *kairos* has preserved the vital content of life, the love of soul for soul, and the love of soul for God. This is the distinctive contribution of the Judaeo-Christian civilization, and Browning makes the point clearly in *Rabbi Ben Ezra*, which first appeared in *Dramatis Personae* (1864):

> Earth changes, but thy soul and God stand sure:
> What entered into thee,
> *That* was, is, and shall be:
> Time's wheel runs back or stops: Potter and clay endure.

Man's being, the core of it in his soul, has been shaped by the Creator, and redeemed by the Son, and so shares the ontological fulness of the being of God himself. Rabbi Ben Ezra, who in youth saw the power of God, in his age can "see now Love perfect too." Thus the rabbi can commit his times (the biblical *chronoi*) into God's hands because they are fleeting; he has seen "the whole design . . . by a spark" that marks the *kairos* or revelatory moment. The lovers in *Love Among the Ruins* have experienced the same revelatory *kairos* of love, and it has redeemed time for them, and has set the ruins of the past into their proper perspective. Browning does not say that the city's good was to provide the ruins for the revelatory moment, but he does hold that the love now flourishing where there had only been power and beauty before is better than anything that the city could offer.

In *Love Among the Ruins* there was action on the part of the lovers and the moment of happiness was secured, but in *The Statue and the Bust* (in *Men and Women*, 1855) there is no action, and the good minute is lost. The duke and the lady look at one another, but that is all. The look is the lady's last free act, because she is immured in her chamber, there to lament her life, and she cannot bring herself to escape from her prison. Browning's comment on the poem is interesting. He condemns the inaction and foresees that in heaven these lovers who did not act on the stimulus of their love will not see God. The good minute must be seized and used if it is to redeem time. The privilege of the sight of God is reserved for

> The soldier-saints who, row on row,
> Burn upward each to his point of bliss—
> Since, the end of his life being manifest,
> He had burned his way through the world to this.

The reference to the soldier-saints is important, and one that Browning made thematic in *The Ring and the Book*, where Caponsacchi is regarded as the soldier-saint (as in the last lines of Pompilia's monologue). The image combines the Perseus-and-Andromeda symbol with that of Saint George, and is representative of chivalric love. The soldier-saint has dared to love, and has acted on that love to catch the good minute. In Browning love is always associated with his feelings for Elizabeth Barrett Browning, and it is clear that Browning regarded himself as something of the soldier-saint in carrying Elizabeth off as the victorious lover. His wife thus raises simultaneously the emotions of religion and love and art in Browning's response. His debt to his wife in religion, so clear from *Christmas-Eve and Easter-Day* on, is balanced by his regard for her own accomplishments as a poet (he always regarded her achievement as greater than his own). But it is in the remarkably pure and intimate love relationship between them that the greatest debt to Elizabeth is acknowledged in poem after poem by Browning. His wife thus combines the main themes that we have been considering in this examination of Browning's monologues, but Browning never saw his poetic task as simply to analyse his wife in poetic terms. He had to analyse himself, and see there what his wife had contributed to his own active life. In the poem written after Mrs. Browning's death, *Prospice*, Browning speaks of his attitude to death as that of a soldier, surrounded by his peers, "the heroes of old," ready for the last battle lasting a "black minute." After the battle, the symbols of immortality crowd in. Browning's favourite symbol for his wife and her love, a light or star, will illuminate all, and the souls of the lovers will be joined in heaven as they were on earth. The difference between earth and heaven will not be in quality or quantity of the love, but in the mode of existence. In heaven the lovers will be enjoying the unity and wholeness of vision that comes from the delight in perfect love—perfect love in each other and perfect love in God. Time will be eternity and the moment will be all in all. It is a glimpse of this ultimate reality that illuminates the lovers of *Love Among the Ruins*; it is a yearning for this reality that informs *Prospice*.

Two in the Campagna provides a marked contrast with *Love Among the Ruins*. It is closer in theme to *The Statue and the Bust*, but in *Two in the Campagna* the lovers do not seize the good minute at all. They suffer the "pain of finite hearts that yearn." The lover strives to hold fast to the love that motivates him, but the barrier of the two selves seems to interrupt the insight that should be shared. The lovers cannot merge their separate personalities in a self-giving of soul to soul. For a moment it seems that the barrier between the lovers is about to vanish. The speaker desires to will through his beloved's will, see through her eyes, and love through her heart, but the yearning for union remains only yearning. Then all seems to be slipping into the past. The yearning can itself be remembered as something to be cherished, but it is a poor substitute indeed for the real insight:

> I pluck the rose
> And love it more than tongue can speak—
> Then the good minute goes.
>
> Already how am I so far
> Out of that minute?

The speaker does not have a "friendly star" of love and of inspiration to be a beacon to his wandering life as Browning had his "moon of poets" (*One Word More*, XVIII). A primary means of knowledge is denied to him, "just when I seemed about to learn." Love seemed to be about to become eternity, but the selves of the lovers interfered. Love as a mode of knowledge is lost; the illumination is gone. The place of individuality which Browning so much cherished as the heritage of the Incarnation has in this poem been erected into selfishness instead of true selfhood. The love which comes from incarnational individuality gives all, gives up all, and forgives all. That is the action of the self that is required and demanded by love, both divine and human, and in the completion of the action is the union of the lover and the beloved. It takes place in a realm above time so that time is suspended and the moment becomes eternity. The union is mystical and sacramental, pervading all life, and therefore all reality, because of its analogue in the union of the human and the divine in the Incarnation. But the lovers in *Two in the Campagna* remain *two*; they cannot give all and give up all; their selves interfere, and so they lose all.

Browning's study of the perfect integration of the good minute is provided in a magnificent poem, *By the Fireside*, from *Men and Women* (1855). The speaker is meditating in his later years on the love that he had lived with for so long. It has become for him a mode of knowledge; it motivates his actions, and ennobles his being. He speaks from the November of life, and paints a beautiful alpine scene of natural prodigality. Again we are on the mountains of *A Grammarian*, but now we see the life of significant love laid out before us as much as possible.

The mountain scene is the mere preface to the thought which takes the speaker from "my perfect wife, my Leonor" to the moments that they share of mutual understanding. Their hearts and souls are one, and they move on in even greater intimacy:

> My own, see where the years conduct!
> At first, 't was something our two souls
> Should mix as mists do; each is sucked
> In each now: on, the new stream rolls,
> Whatever rocks obstruct.

The doctrine of progress has its contribution to make in the developing love. The speaker looks to the future in a burst of spiritual insight, and there sees the complete reliance of love in this life upon the love of God. When that love is finally consummated in the Judgment, then the love of men will go from depth to depth in the divine love:

> Think, when our one soul understands
> The great Word which makes all things new,
> When earth breaks up and heaven expands,
> How will the change strike me and you
> In the house not made with hands?

The same reference to the heavenly mansions of II Corinthians 5:1 is made by Abt Vogler. In the strength of their love, the two-made-one will grow still more in love. That is the perfect circle of love, the arc of which had been glimpsed by Abt Vogler. The thought is awe-inspiring, even to the speakers, who did not consider that such love and insight were possible:

> But who could have expected this
> When we two drew together first
> Just for the obvious human bliss,
> To satisfy life's daily thirst
> With a thing men seldom miss?

It is a natural step to recall the first blossoming of love, which so often takes the form of physical attraction, but then is sublimated into spiritual union which, upon contemplation, becomes a mode of knowledge. Again the speaker paints a beautiful landscape, the same one as the first, and one more we find ourselves in the middle of another quest for the moment and the peace it can bring. When the moment is least expected, it comes:

> Oh moment, one and infinite!
>> The water slips o'er stock and stone;
> The West is tender, hardly bright:
>> How grey at once is the evening grown—
> One star, its chrysolite!

Again rises the star of Browning's love for Elizabeth (as in the poems *My Star, Christmas-Eve, One Word More, Pompilia,* and a galaxy of others), while nature continues in its course, although transformed by the vision too, just as we saw at the end of *Saul.* The speaker meditates on the exactitude of the moment—how a little more is added to the ordinary love-experience and in a flash eternity is seen; how a little less and the flash would be worlds away. If the will of the beloved had intervened, then the barrier of selfish flesh would have remained (as it did in *Two in the Campagna*), and the two would have been ever two friends, never one love. But the soul of each had pierced "its fine flesh-stuff":

> A moment after, and hands unseen
>> Were hanging the night around us fast;
> But we knew that a bar was broken between
>> Life and life: we were mixed at last
> In spite of the mortal screen.

The same thought is expressed in the poem which follows *By the Fireside* in the first volume of *Men and Women, Any Wife to Any Husband,* but the tone has shifted to irony:

> But now, because the hour through years was fixed,
> Because our inmost beings met and mixed,
>> Because thou once hast loved me—wilt thou dare
> Say to thy soul and Who may list beside,
> "Therefore she is immortally my bride;
> Chance cannot change my love, nor time impair."

The lover in *By the Fireside* realizes that earthly existence is the testing place of the soul to see if it can love well and wisely, while the after-life is a series of progressions from love to Love. The uniqueness of the moment is, in a sense, a test of its validity, underlining the absolute uniqueness of the moment of God's revelatory love in the Incarnation. Browning is denying that there can be love in man apart from God's love, just as there cannot be being in man apart from the being of God which is pure act. Because the pure act of God is most characteristically seen in love, so man's most pure act of being is the act of love, since then he is fulfilling his created and redeemed image. The Incarnation establishes complete relationships, and the moment of love's revelation between man and woman, in that it is a sharing of and incorporation into the love of the Incarnation, also establishes complete relationships:

> I am named and known by that moment's feat;
> There took my station and degree;
> So grew my own small life complete,
> As nature obtained her best of me—
> One born to love you, sweet!

Man's establishment as an individual is accomplished in the Incarnation when he is named the son of God; and so the lover is named and known as an individual in the moment of union in selfless love. Wholeness or, in theological terms, redemption is the result.

Browning and his wife had acted on the evidence of their love in the moment of critical choice (unlike the characters in *The Statue and the Bust*), and eternity hung in the balance. The love of soul for soul broke down the flesh that separated the lovers, and the love of God established a new individuality, replacing the two separate ones which had previously existed. Writing from the interpretation of his own experience, Browning had developed a rather existential doctrine of love that he applied to test experience, and so to test life. The individualism which he had found in the Incarnation as the first crisis of history, and again in the Renaissance as the second crisis, is to be merged in unselfish love for another in the crisis moment of this present life, and in love for God in the next. Even in human life love is seen as the expression of the infinite love of God. Its presence in the human heart is one of the best assurances to Browning of the divine existence, an avenue to belief that he had examined in *A Death in the Desert*. For Browning it is not merely possible, nor even just probable that God exists; it is an existential and psychological necessity; nevertheless, one must still doubt if one is to strive. Browning had developed his theory of love in much wider contexts than the merely physical. He related the moment of religious experience which the saint may experience in the desert to the moment of artistic inspiration cherished by the poet or painter or musician, and to the moment of union in physical bliss between lovers. David's love for Saul had been characterized by an infinite and unselfish benevolence which received its supreme example in the love of Christ, seen in a vision at the end of the monologue. In lovers there must also be unselfishness, and that is the out-going attribute of *caritas*, the direction of the will towards the highest good. Thus the self is not only transcended, but is sublimated in love. The love of man is exalted, and the self of God reaches down; and in the result the finitude of self is stamped with the infinity of God, the *imago Dei*, in the Incarnation.

Browning's doctrine of love is very close to St. Augustine's, not only as examined above in the discussion of the Trinity and the three faculties of power, knowledge, and love as attributes of the three souls. Augustine uses three terms for love, *amor*, *caritas*, and *cupiditas*. Love is motivated by *amor appetitus* (unfulfilled desire) and it moves upwards by degrees to love something higher. *Amor* refers to love in general, as the appreciation and desire for beautiful things; it is the driving psychological force; and above all it directs the will towards the Good, the True, the Beautiful, and the Desirable. *Caritas* is Christian charity, holding the object of love as a treasure, and seeing the treasure as impelling an ordering of life on the way of perfection to God. Here is the fruition of *caritas*. *Cupiditas* is the self-seeking and self-directed grasping love of misdirected *amor*.[3] It is the sin of cupidity, greedy desire, and the mere satisfaction of the appetites. It is *amor* which has been corrupted by pride.

In the light of the doctrine of love held by St. Augustine, Browning's doctrine is seen to be consistent. To show the interconnection of the different threads of thought, the aspects of love and life that we have been examining, we could assemble Browning's monologues in a diagram. The religious, art, and love monologues can be related in the same scheme, and properly may be oriented to the governing concept of love in the Incarnation. Robert Browning himself is the focal centre of the scheme which we have been presenting (and so he is properly the centre of the diagram). His religious views, formulated and strengthened in *Christmas-Eve and Easter-Day*, find expression in the whole range of religious experience from Caliban to Gigadibs. But always it is the Incarnation which remains the central doctrine, and Elizabeth Barrett is the one who drew him to it. The monologues on painting and music elaborate the same themes in artistic terms (love and

[3]Huizinga in his *Waning of the Middle Ages* writes: "Medieval doctrine found the root of all evil either in the sin of pride or in cupidity. . . . It seems, nevertheless, that from the twelfth century downward people begin to find the principle of evil rather in cupidity than in pride. The voices which condemn blind cupidity, 'la cieca cupidigia' of Dante, become louder and louder" (27).

the philosophy of the imperfect), while those on love itself analyse the presence of eternity in a moment of vision. And always for Browning there still "burns the central truth":

> Within whose circle of experience burns
> The central truth, Power, Wisdom, Goodness,—God.
>
> (*The Ring and the Book,* X, 1632–3)

A conflict which seemed to be arising between the love of God and the sensual love of the sexes may be explained by means of Augustine's emphasis on the place of will. Browning would place an equal stress on it in the moment of critical choice when the will must be motivated by true love. *Amor* directs the will to the Good; *caritas* orders life to become the Good Life, the *Summum Bonum*. For Browning *amor* would lead to the critical moment and would direct the will to act. It remains for *caritas* to order life to the attainment of perfection in love. Benevolence then becomes a part of willing the good, and that is as far as David can get in his attitude towards Saul in the first version of the poem without the gift of Christian *caritas*. So it is with Browning himself. He needed his Beatrice Portinari to guide him from the love of earth to the love of heaven.[4] That Browning regarded Elizabeth as his Beatrice, we know from *One Word More*:

> Oh, their Dante of the dread Inferno,
> Wrote one song—and in my brain I sing it,
> Drew one angel—borne, see, on my bosom!

Other connections drew Browning and Dante together—Florence, Giotto, love, theology, and poetry—but above all it was the cherishing of the beloved, both in love as the means of full expression, and after the beloved's death, as the means of poetic and religious inspiration. Again and again Browning is motivated by what Dante calls "*d'antico amor . . . la gran potenza*" (*Purgatorio*, xxx, 39) and is able to continue to address his love in *Prospice*, and the *Epilogue* to *Dramatis Personae*, and

---

[4]Cf. Huizinga in his *Waning of the Middle Ages*: "Without giving up all connection with sensual love, the new poetic ideal was capable of embracing all kinds of ethical aspirations. Love now became the field where all moral and cultural perfection flowered. Because of his love, the courtly lover is pure and virtuous. The spiritual element dominates more and more, till towards the end of the thirteenth century, the *dolce stil nuovo* of Dante and his friends ends by attributing to love the gift of bringing about a state of piety and holy intuition" (107).

later in *Ferishtah's Fancies.*[5] Love for Browning, as for St. Augustine, is higher than the moral order, although it may impose a pattern upon the moral order. Love is the prime theological virtue, and so it is in Dante. Those in Purgatory have defective, excessive, or perverse love, derived from the seven deadly sins in the moral order. The theological virtues of faith, hope, and love are reserved for the *Paradiso*, and are particularly shown in Beatrice. In Browning too love is part of the order of grace, and so it is presented in the religious monologues, the art poetry, and the love lyrics. The contexts are different, and different aspects of the phenomenon are exposed to our eyes and minds; but all are part of Browning's ceaseless inquiry into the meaning of the Incarnation in men's lives.

[5]Browning had achieved with Dante *"sua vita nuova"* (*Purgatorio*, xxx, 115; and cf. the *Vita Nuova* itself) by means of love which is greater and includes power and knowledge:
Fecemi la divina potestate
La somma sapienza, e 'l primo amore.
The lines were also favourites of Tennyson's, as Hallam tells us (*Tennyson*, I, 322).

COMPOSITE UNITY:
THE RING AND THE BOOK

For many a doubt will fain perturb my choice—
Many a dream of life spent otherwise—
How human love, in varied shapes, might work
As glory, or as rapture, or as grace: . . .
. . . It is the glory and good of Art,
That Art remains the one way possible
Of speaking truth, to mouths like mine at least.

(*The Ring and the Book*, XII, 625–7, 842–4)

I. THE RING OF TRUTH

In the lines from the prophetic conclusion to his first major poem, *Pauline* (1833), Browning presents a number of themes which are to be reworked again and again throughout his life. These themes reach their most perfect expression in the greatest literary monument of Victorian England, *The Ring and the Book*. But Browning was still not satisfied or finished with his treatment of these themes, and he continued with *Fifine, La Saisiaz,* on through the *Parleyings with Certain People* to *Asolando: Fancies and Facts,* published on December 12, 1889, the day of Browning's death. His life shows a remarkable consistency as the same principles are enunciated, and the same agonizing struggle to relate them to experience suffered again and again. In the lines from *Pauline* we notice that the poet is going to rise through the darkness into light (a constant image in Browning, connecting his literary activity with Elizabeth Barrett, and especially useful to him in *The Ring and the Book*) where he will see more clearly, love better, and trumpet belief in God, truth, and love. After all is said, these ideas comprise the single unified theme of the whole poem, combining religion, art, and love in the poetic activity. The poem is the almost-nine-years' distillation of his abiding interests sublimated into his quintessential vision of what Fra Celestino in the last pages of the poem calls "a dream of life." It is a vision addressed to the "British Public, ye who like me not," but "who may like me yet," and it is patently didactic:

> . . . learn one lesson hence
> Of many which whatever lives should teach:
> This lesson, that our human speech is naught,
> Our human testimony false, our fame
> And human estimation words and wind.
>
> (XII, 836–40)

Life is to be used, as Browning sees it, and he explains in *La Saisiaz*:

> Life has worth incalculable, every moment that he spends
> So much gain or loss for that next life which on this life depends.
> Good, done here, be there rewarded,—evil worked here, there amerced!
>
> (477–9)

The vision of a dream of life-which-is-used is not the only thing in *The Ring and the Book*. "Least part this—then what the whole?" The "whole" involves Browning's views of God, truth, and love as expressed in the dream of life. In *The Ring and the Book* there is a special way of teaching this doctrine, and again it is at the end of the poem where we find so many of his principles, that this one, implied throughout, is made explicit.

> . . . it is the glory and good of Art,
> That Art remains the one way possible
> Of speaking truth . . . Art may tell a truth
> Obliquely, do the thing shall breed the thought,
> Nor wrong the thought, missing the mediate word.
>
> (XII, 842, 859)

For this reason Browning can "write a book" which "shall mean beyond the facts,/Suffice the eye and save the soul beside" (XII, 866–7). Art, then, as in the Renaissance monologues like *Fra Lippo Lippi* or *Andrea Del Sarto*, is representative of life, and through art we may arrive at truth.

Pilate asked "What is truth?" and Browning echoes him as he attempts to provide a partial answer, and at least one way of approaching truth. The titular symbol of the ring is at least the first key to unlock the poem's riddle. Some critics have felt that the metaphor is adequate; some have praised while others have condemned it; even DeVane thinks that "Browning presses the figure too far."[1] However, if one accepts it for what it is, an ingeniously developed and subtly clever unifying symbol of the poem's themes, then Browning is surely justified in his use of it.

"Do you see this Ring?" the poem begins, and we soon realize that it is the same question as Pilate's. The ring has a number of obvious meanings. It is the tangible manifestation of the love of Browning and Elizabeth Barrett because it is the ring which she wore. McAleer records the history of the ring in his edition of Browning's letters to Isabella Blagden, *Dearest Isa*:

Isa presented each of the Brownings with a ring made by the Roman jeweller Castellani. EBB's was inscribed ΑΕΙ, the Greek for "eternally," and she acknowledged it with the following note (MS in BM): "I can't wait till to-night to thank you my dearest Isa for this exquisite little ring—shall I not keep it for ever, as a memorial of what must last as long,—my true love for you, *dear*? Oh—I like it so much better than any 'Aurora' in the world. . . ." (11, n. 5)

Cook, in his *Commentary*, gives us the subsequent history: "Mr. R. Barrett Browning has written as follows: 'The ring was of Etruscan shape made by Castellani, which my mother wore. On it are the letters Α Ε Ι. Ever after her death my father wore it on his watch chain'" (7, n. 1). Browning, then, treasured the ring as a personal and private symbol of his love for and marriage with Elizabeth Barrett. While such a symbol is significant, still "least part this: then what the whole?"

The ring has an artistic and less private meaning. It is a symbol of the work of art, of its totality, its completeness. Furthermore, it is the symbol of poetic truth because of its use as a metaphor, and because of the meanings which Browning gives to its ingredients. It represents the artifact, the poetic and creative act, the highest attainable form of human truth, even the symbolic expression of Divine truth. Here, then, in the ring symbol are caught up those three affirmations from *Pauline*—

---

[1]*Handbook*, 330. An extensive discussion is found in J. B. McElderry, "Victorian Evaluation of *The Ring and the Book*," *Research Studies of the State College of Washington*, June, 1939.

belief "in God and truth and love"—and all do, in the symbol as in actuality, achieve a unity in the perfection of the ring's form.

But there is still more to it. The ring is a geometric pattern which because of its solidity and mass, has something of the sphere in it. The sphere has been a symbol for Divine truth for centuries. It is made up of the countless circles of perfection which are God; of these, there are three main ones, depicted in art as three intersecting circles representing the three Persons of the Trinity. The single circle is the symbol for poetic truth, that truth which the poet as man of vision, as "priest and prophet" in the words of *Pauline*, can see more clearly than other men. Just as there are a limitless number of circles in the perfect sphere, so there are a limitless number of arcs in the perfect circle, and each arc represents limited truth, the half-truth, the truth of the world, the light that we have. Abt Vogler knows the difference between earth's imperfection and heaven's perfections:

> On the earth the broken arcs; in the heaven a perfect round.

The problem becomes multiplied almost indefinitely if we remember the Pope's words in his monologue (and it would be so much easier to forget them, so much less complex to omit them) as he rejects the doubt of salvation:

> I
> Put no such dreadful question to myself,
> Within whose *circle* of experience burns
> The central truth, Power, Wisdom, Goodness,—God.
> (X, 1630–3)

Now we find that we can consider the ring in relation to all of the perfect attributes of God, his omnipotence, omniscience, and omni-benevolence, and the question at the opening of the poem "Do you see this Ring?" is seen in its full ironic light. The possibility of seeing the ring whole and clear is never given to us. We see in moments, in flashes of sudden illumination some part of it; the rest is hidden in eternity. The perfect ring, if we could see it, is the image of eternity. Hence it is also absolute truth, that known only in God's timelessness. But the ring made in time is also an image of the cycle of time itself. Each of its arcs is "one fact the more"—and as the temporal ring is forged of these facts, Browning can add, "one truth the less." The element of truth in the ring imparts its eternal nature; "mere fact" imparts temporality. The ring is the truth held in a suspension of fancy and fact; it is eternity made temporal, or in other words of Browning, it is infinity fitted to the finite. The ring is thus a symbol for the Incarnation, with its combination of all of these paradoxes. The whole poem is cast in the light of the Incarnation. The main characters refer to it in a way which is a touchstone to their personalities. Indeed, the murders themselves took place during the Christmas festival, and much is made of the parallels between the birth of Christ and the birth of Gaetano. The ring of truth is the constant unifying symbol of the poem; its theological significance is the centrality of the Incarnation to the entire poem, coming chiefly to the fore in the Pope's monologue. Browning has used a series of historical events—these are the facts in his fabric—but he has interwoven them with his interpretation. It is one of his great beliefs that facts are never known to man as truth, but must be accompanied with a living interpretation to make the truth shine through them. So it is with the Incarnation; so it is with the ring and the book. In his *Fulness of Time* (159), John Marsh makes the same point:

The truth is that "facts of history," like "sensa" in human perception, are never known to us save as interpreted and related to other facts in history. Knowledge or experience of the historical presupposes *both* fact *and* the interpretation of the fact. But neither must we suppose that interpretations are given in abstraction from historical facts, any more than true perceptions can be given which are not bound up with data really present to the senses. For the historian this means that his interpretation must not proceed solely from *a priori* philosophical principles, but be derived from the process of history itself. These twin considerations are of considerable importance to the Christian theologian, for his faith prescribes that his understanding of history must always begin from certain facts-with-interpretations (such as "the Cross"), and yet his interpretation of history must be integrally related to certain public events of history—as the recital of the classic creeds of the Church continually shows.

"Fact-with-interpretation" is the same kind of attempt to get at a convenient means of expressing truth as Browning's composite symbol.

Browning's infinite variety will not let us stop even here in our exploration of his ring metaphor. From the very beginning Browning concentrates much of his emphasis on the materials of the ring:

> The artificer . . . mingles gold
> With gold's alloy, and, duly tempering both,
> Effects a manageable mass, then works:
> But his work ended, once the thing a ring,

Oh, there's repristination! Just a spirt
O' the proper fiery acid o'er its face,
And forth the alloy unfastened flies in fume.

(I, 18–24)

So the ring is made, and is purified by means of the acid. The alloy,
which held the ring in shape while it was being worked is removed
from sight:

While, self-sufficient now, the shape remains,
The rondure brave, the lilied loveliness,
Gold as it was, is, shall be evermore:
Prime nature with an added artistry—
No carat lost, and you have gained a ring.
What of it? 'Tis a figure, a symbol, say;
A thing's sign: now for the thing signified.

(I, 26–32)

Browning explains that "the thing signified" is truth and fact and fancy
and fiction, each quite definitely in its place, but the embodiment given
to the symbol in *The Ring and the Book* begins to be shown to us through
the other titular symbol, the book. "Do you see this square old yellow
Book?" asks Browning and again the irony challenges the reader in
his complacency with the same kind of question as was asked about
the ring.

Here it is, this I toss and take again;
Small-quarto size, part print, part manuscript:
A book in shape but, really, pure crude fact
Secreted from man's life. . . .   (I, 84–87)

So here it is, the composite symbol of ring and book both interlocking,
if that be possible, one with the other. The *Old Yellow Book*, or the
primary source, which Browning found,

(Mark the predestination!) when a Hand,
Always above my shoulder, pushed me once,
One day still fierce 'mid many a day struck calm,
Across a Square in Florence, crammed with booths,

(I, 40–3)

contained "a Roman murder-case" which was the "pure crude fact."
However the *Old Yellow Book* contained more than "fanciless fact" for
"in this book lay absolutely truth." He sums up so far:

> This is the bookful; thus far take the truth,
> The untempered gold, the fact untampered with,
> The mere ring-metal ere the ring be made!
>
> (I, 364–6)

Fact then is the gold ore which contains truth and pure tempered gold within it. Browning had to dig (and dig it must have been, for he says that he read the *Old Yellow Book* eight times during the nine-years' time which occupied the writing of the poem):

> . . . thence bit by bit I dug
> The lingot truth, that memorable day,
> Assayed, and knew my piecemeal gain was gold. . . .
>
> (I, 458–60)

But life is short, no matter how long art is, and Browning had to forge his ring by means of something added to the gold:

> Yes; but from something else surpassing that,
> Something of mine which, mixed up with the mass,
> Made it bear hammer and be firm to file.
>
> (I, 461–3)

What did he add?

> Fancy with fact is just one fact the more;
> To wit, that fancy has informed, transpierced,
> Thridded and so thrown fast the facts else free,
> As right through ring and ring runs the djereed
> And binds the loose, one bar without a break.
> I fused my live soul and that inert stuff,
> Before attempting smithcraft, on the night
> After the day when,—truth thus grasped and gained,—
> The book was shut and done with and laid by.
>
> (I, 464–72)

Browning's fancy, the poet's creative imagination, transforms the "mere fact" into a greater truth in fiction. In a poem written ten years later, *The Two Poets of Croisic*, Browning explains somewhat more fully:

> But truth, truth, that's the gold! and all the good
>   I find in fancy is, it serves to set
> Gold's inmost glint free, gold which comes up rude
>   And rayless from the mine. All fume and fret
> Of artistry beyond this point pursued
>   Brings out another sort of burnish: yet

> Always the ingot has its very own
> Value, a sparkle struck from truth alone.
>
> (CLII, 1209–16)

Browning's fancy is represented in the ring metaphor as the alloy:

> . . . such alloy
> Such substance of me interfused the gold
> Which, wrought into a shapely ring therewith,
> Hammered and filed, fingered and favoured, last
> Lay ready for the renovating wash
> O' the water.   (I, 681–6)

Here Browning becomes intensely ironic as he asks Pilate's question once more, but in more direct words than "Do you see this ring or book?":

> "How much of the tale was true?" (I, 686)

His answer is even more ironic:

> I disappeared; the book grew all in all . . .
> Lovers of dead truth, did ye fare the worse?
> Lovers of live truth, found ye false my tale?
>
> (I, 687–9)

The reader must answer Browning's questions somehow or other because the decree of the Pope (and of Browning) is really "the ultimate judgment save yours." Gold, as a most precious metal, is paradoxically the most valueless unless the creative imagination of both the reader and the poet can hammer the gold with its alloy into usable shape. Then "fiery acid" is used with superb irony as the surface of the ring becomes gold, while underneath is the alloy inextricably mixed with the gold. That is, we have Browning and his fancy-alloy with us constantly in the poem to interpret, expand, comment, guide, or influence, always by means of his poetic imagination. The poet is, like the poor, always with us.

The Roman murder-case seemed significant to Browning, no doubt, because at a number of points it closely paralleled his own life (especially in the Perseus–Andromeda–St. George legend, which will be treated later). There is abundant evidence for the belief that Browning constantly read himself into the poem. For example, he consistently referred to it in his letters as "RB," the same initials as his own name. When Browning looks at life (his own, or that of his characters) he sees a narrative which carries with it a meaning and a moral. In *The Ring and the Book* he has the "providential" means of interpreting an intrinsically interesting narrative, which is thereby given meaning. He has complete liberty to supply motivation which was not in the case itself so that we may ourselves evaluate the moral and establish the meaning.

To understand Browning's ring is to hold in one's mind a similar figure, the golden branch of Venus given to Aeneas for his journey in Virgil's sixth book. Both will provide safe conduct through a Hades which, without them, would become a Valley of the Shadow of Death. The ring and book provide the key to the structure of the whole poem, and through them the whole becomes meaningful. Truth, not acted upon by the imagination, remains "pure crude fact" and is without use, but it has immediate value if it is used, especially if it is used to enlighten life. In *The Ring and the Book* the meaning comes from the characters themselves since they express or betray their own motives, their view of truth, and their view of life. That is to say that the "truth" of the poem is a reading of life. Life must be acted upon by the imagination, or else life slips back into fact, that is, mere existence. Life must be seen in its greater reality too, as related to the nature of God. The Pope's "Power, Wisdom, Goodness," "the central truth" and its meaning in life had been explained over thirty years before as Paracelsus attained:

> Power—neither put forth blindly, nor controlled
> Calmly by perfect knowledge; to be *used*
> At risk, inspired or checked by hope and fear:
> Knowledge—not intuition, but the slow
> Uncertain fruit of an enhancing toil,
> Strengthened by love: love—not serenely pure
> But strong from weakness, . . .   (V, 693–9)

These aspects of truth itself have their meaning when used as Paracelsus says, but the use is often difficult and the meaning doubtful. Nevertheless, even Sordello is very much aware of these things,

> such peace-in-strife
> By transmutation, is the Use of Life . . .
> (III, 166–7)

It is the function of the poet to "impart the gift of seeing to the rest" (*Sordello*, III, 868), to teach the "Use of Life," to show truth. In *The*

Ring and the Book this task of the poet is admirably fulfilled. Browning saw the task as one for both the subjective and the objective poet. In his *Essay on Shelley* he writes what may be applied with great relevance to the artist's creative act in *The Ring and the Book.* He argues that the objective poet has the

double faculty of seeing external objects more clearly, widely, and deeply than is possible to the average mind, at the same time that he is so acquainted and in sympathy with its narrower comprehension as to be careful to supply it with no other materials than it can combine into an intelligible whole. . . . The subjective poet . . . , gifted like the objective poet with the fuller perception of nature and man, is impelled to embody the thing he perceives, not so much with reference to the many below as to the one above him, the supreme Intelligence which apprehends all things in their absolute truth,—an ultimate view ever aspired to, if but partially attained, by the poet's own soul. Not what man sees, but what God sees. . . .

This is the task of Browning as poet as well as the task of the Pope as judge. The Pope's discussion of Euripides underlines the connection between the poet, the judge, and the priest. All have to interpret what they have seen of the vision of truth. But the creative act in the poet is different from the creative act of God. God creates *ex nihilo*, and since man must use God's creation, and God's truth, man can only participate with God in an act of re-creation. Thus man must use the gold of truth which is given him in time to make the meaningful ring, "Till, justifiably golden, rounds my ring" (I, 1389). Still, Browning asks, "A ring without a posy, and that ring mine?," and makes reply by addressing his "Lyric Love." At the end of the poem he returns to the same love when the trial, the judgments ("save yours"), and the executions are finished. The circle of the poem is complete (as shown by the inversion of Book I's title for Book XII), and this posy, this ring, this Book, is complete:

> If the rough ore be rounded to a ring,
> Render all duty which good ring should do,
> And, failing grace, succeed in guardianship,—
> Might mine but lie outside thine, Lyric Love,
> Thy rare gold ring of verse (the poet praised)
> Linking our England to his Italy!
>
> (XII, 869–74)

In Book I Browning achieves a variety of tonal effect, but, as always, there is a purpose behind the variety. He is building up the structure of the ring symbol to combine his interests in painting, music, religion, love, and poetry, so that he will have a means of relating them to his unique effort in the structure of the dramatic monologue. He is using the ring as the type of the creative intuition informed by love, and endowed with all of the craftsman's skill; the flash of acid over the surface is the creative moment, and the capturing of the moment is the effort of the poem's structure. In *Abt Vogler* Browning had examined the nature of the moment of creative intuition and had seen the analogous nature of the Incarnation; in the love poetry he had applied the creative moment to love as it gives an illuminative impetus to life. Now in *The Ring and the Book* Browning is ready to examine his own adventure into the communication of simultaneous experience. That is why he is able to tell the whole of the poem's dramatic story in thirty lines in Book I (780–823), so that if one is reading the poem for the story, one need go no further than the first ten pages where it is all told. Browning is then free to present the different accounts, focusing his attention on thousands of different details, and yet relating all of them to the plot outline. The disclosure of the story gives his ample ironic vein all of the room that it needs to unfold as he allows the characters to introduce themselves. Here is the creative moment in the poem—as the acid from our minds, our own intuition, works on the poem's matter, and tries to extract the truth from the ore. We see the characters after Guido had faced his own moment of critical choice, but that very action imposes a decision on our own minds. The poet too is engaged in the setting forth of the simultaneous critical moments in each of the *personae* and so each of the books is a separate examination of the creative intuition of the poet engaged in his distinctive activity. If his work can make us see some glimmer of truth through the mediate words of his art, then he will have succeeded to the rank of highest poets, the "Makers-see." Illuminative truth, which had been the ultimate goal of all of the poetry, is made the explicit goal of *The Ring and the Book*. Immediately after the plot-summary in Book I, Browning inserts a short and important paragraph. In parentheses (where the poet so often in the poetry makes valuable comment *in propria persona*, as in the important parentheses in *A Death in the Desert*, where the same material is inserted) he asks:

> (. . . how heart moves brain and how both move hand,
> What mortal ever in entirety saw?)　　　　(I, 828)

Again here is the tripartite division in man of God's attributes of power, knowledge, and love. Then Browning links these attributes, as he had done in the discussion of the three souls in *A Death in the Desert*, with the Incarnation, asking "how else know we save by worth of word?" He is referring to the word made flesh, the poetic word from the *Old Yellow Book* turned into the flesh of his monologuists, as well as to the governing root of the idea in the Word of God in whose light alone the poet's words have significance. It is important that here at such a crucial juncture in the first book, just after the summary of the action, a reference to the attributes of God and the Incarnation is introduced to show the true centre of objective truth. Truth is more than the vision of it reveals, and so the ultimate irony is that truth is never wholly seen, and that the ring is never wholly finished. Because each speaker judges the facts himself by his own light, then each is indulging in a creative act which is at least in part true. Yet Browning has implicitly judged the validity of the speakers' views even before he writes. The whole poem can thus take on its most appropriate ironic colour.

Browning has adopted psychological suspense instead of dramatic as the medium for the poem's dramatic story, and variety is maintained as each speaker selects a different aspect of the plot and the detail to receive emphasis in his part of the poem. Thus, although the story itself is retold at least eleven times, the detail is carefully manipulated to illuminate a different facet of the truth of life. Browning is making his most valiant effort to present the reader with a simultaneous view of life, so that the difficulties of poetic structure that he had discussed in *Sordello* are partially resolved. The whole poem can be seen in its various aspects and in its depth only when finished, but even from the first chronicle of events, an illusion of simultaneity is created. The reader is left to concentrate upon Browning's interpretation of the action. We are presented with only one of the engrossing minds at a time, and so each group of the motivations, each set of variations on a theme, can be developed extensively with breath-taking singleness of purpose. The unity of the poem comes from its great concept of truth, symbolized in the ring, and from its narrative and architectural structure.

The poem's twelve books are carefully arranged so that there is a general introduction in the first book; the central nine books comprise a triple trilogy; then Guido speaks a second time, and the last book draws the remaining threads together in a kind of epilogue. In each group of three monologues in the central nine books, the first speaker is a Guido supporter, while the second supports Pompilia. Both of these groups represent biased views or special pleadings. The third speaker, somewhat removed from party loyalties, looks on things with a certain detachment and objectivity. "Tertium Quid" suffers from a false detachment; Pompilia has a genuine disinterestedness; and the Pope is as impartially objective as it is possible for man to be. The first speaker in each group is a husband, the second a bachelor or celibate, and the third is again more objective in being removed from sexual connotations (although this is false too in "Tertium Quid"). The pattern of climax follows the structural lines of the triple trilogy. Thus Browning, whose custom is to think in threes (the Trinity; power, knowledge, love; the three souls; and so on), can develop the individuality of each character in a setting of psychological suspense where each is forced to interact with other characters. The pattern of climax, then, is related to the idea that Browning has of the poem's simultaneity. There can be several climaxes, each one fitted to the organic structure of the individual trilogy, but there must also be a master climax which governs the whole movement of the poem. The structural pattern of narrative and climax is a pattern which derives its form from the arrangement of the characters themselves and from the complexities of the time scheme. When the poem's master climax comes in the Pope's monologue, then it is suitable that the controlling thought of the poem, the centrality of the Incarnation, also should assume its true position. Then the poetic simultaneity which Browning is trying to achieve can be related to the theological simultaneity of the supreme creative moment. Both Pompilia and the Pope deliver their monologues on the thin edge of time, balancing on the brink of eternity. The temporal processes are almost suspended while they speak (another contribution to simultaneity), both ready to "die this very night" (X, 2133). Both have known the blinding flash of love and have lived in it; now they are ready to die in it. The tension of the Pope's monologue is greater from a dramatic standpoint because he sees deeper into the heart of love than Pompilia whose experience was like that recorded in the love lyrics of Browning. The Pope lives in the light of the Incarnation and his critical choice is made through the experience of that unique moment.

The whole poem is also seen in its instantaneous aspect in terms of the ring symbol. With the "flash of acid" the ring is forged, when the poem is finished. Browning has made his most venturesome excursion into an analysis of the minute. Nine lives are summed up and analysed for their interaction as well as for themselves. The poem, no less than Milton's epic, is an attempt "to justify the ways of God to men." The justification takes place in the critical moment, and although we know what the choice of the Pope will be, nevertheless eternity does hang on the moment of critical choice. The Pope acts finally in the objective light of truth, truth revealed in the history of the Incarnation, and subjectively interpreted by himself as he fulfils his vocation to interpret truth to a waiting world. The decision of the Pope depends itself upon the flash of insight. It is the momentary incarnation of truth, and can only come because of the Pope's meditation upon the Incarnation of Love. Again in the poem the past is related to the present:

> Yet, a little while,
> The passage of a century or so,
> Decades thrice five, and here's time paid his tax,
> Oblivion gone home with her harvesting,
> And all left smooth again as scythe could shave.
>
> (I, 417-22)

The poem's place in history is eternally present in the posy that the poet presents for the sake of love to the public; it is eternally present at the core of Browning's poetry as the posy that his love presents (and that is in fact his art, himself, RB) to his Lyric Love.

2. THE PEOPLE OF THE BOOK

After the first three speakers outline the views of the various parties in *The Ring and the Book*, Browning is able to introduce the main characters of the poem. All of the characters are related to the central themes of the Incarnation, time, the centre of truth in its relation to fact, and the interpretation of history. Half-Rome, a Guido-supporter, presents the views of half of the world, "the world's outcry/Around the rush and ripple of any fact . . ." (I, 839). Other Half-Rome presents his own bias of fact and truth by judicially selecting those which he wishes to present. Both Half-Rome and Other Half-Rome have a limited vision, and so they remain on the periphery of truth. Tertium Quid falls between in a morass of indecision. He cannot make the necessary choice which would place him in a time and space relationship to the central characters, the world, or the Pope. Browning uses a constant metaphor to present the attitudes of the characters to the events of the slaying. Half-Rome introduces the metaphor:

> . . . the gallant, Caponsacchi, Lucifer
> I' the garden where Pompilia, Eve-like, lured
> Her Adam Guido to his fault and fall.
> (II, 167–9)

The Eden-comparison is used frequently, as is the idea of Pompilia as a lure. The idea of Eve as a lure is common in patristic theology where it is definitely and finally linked with the Incarnation. When "the Word became flesh," he did so of the purity of the Virgin Mary (the Second Eve). The manhood of Christ which he took of the Virgin was regarded as the bait or lure (in St. Augustine, the mousetrap) which would be paid to the Devil at the Atonement as a ransom. The use of the figure and debate over the receiver of the ransom was a great pastime for the patristic and scholastic mind. In Browning the relation of Pompilia to the Virgin Mary is evident enough, although it is not directly stated. Pompilia is a type of the pure and chaste virgin, a sort of conflation of the imagery associated with Venus and the Virgin in the style of the courtly love tradition. We notice how Browning has each of the characters present his own re-interpretation of the Eden and Virgin metaphor. Half-Rome picks up the image as he describes Violante's treacherous action as she

> . . . threw her bait, Pompilia, where he sulked—
> A gleam i' the gloom!   (II, 323)

Here Half-Rome has neatly combined the lure image and the light image in the description of Pompilia.

Another area of imagery which is a touchstone for Browning's thought in *The Ring and the Book* is the treatment of truth and fact by each of the characters. Truth and fact usually apply to the interpretation of time and the attitude to history which is held by each character. Half-Rome begins his account of Guido by echoing the "pure crude fact" given by Browning in Book I, but soon the colouring tarnishes truth (II, 278) just as it does with his treatment of Caponsacchi (II, 695). He beats his drum soundly:

> But facts are facts and flinch not; stubborn things . . .
> (II, 1049)

and his conviction about his own view of truth is equally certain:

> You take your stand on truth ere leap your lie:
> Here was all lie, no touch of truth at all,
> All the lie here.   (II, 554–6)

We see what he has done. He has examined what facts he wished, and, adding his fancy to them, has seen just what he wished to prove, "wanting to prove, if proof consoles at all" (II, 1077). Pompilia is described as (and the irony is that the description is right) "terrible as truth," and over her the law (the natural law, not God's, as Half-Rome protests) must triumph:

> Let law shine forth and show, as God in heaven,
> Vice prostrate, virtue pedestalled at last,
> The triumph of truth.   (II, 1085–7)

So does the half-world look on truth, and see sensationalism, much as Gigadibs had seen it, as the facts which supposedly "flinch not" are violently twisted. Half-Rome takes the same delight in the deceit and treachery of Violante's action found out through the confessional that Browning had so much earlier explored in one of his first and most melodramatic monologues, *Soliloquy of the Spanish Cloister*. Half-Rome is revealed in his attitude to the moment, because it is truth or fact which is to be seen in the moment. He has seen the evidence in the church, and he has judged with "certainty," never doubting:

> . . . one sees indeed
> Not only how all was and must have been,
> But cannot other than be to the end of time.
>   (II, 185–7)

The rest of the world, in the person of Other Half-Rome, errs in a like manner by seeing only the other half of the picture. The hushed, reverential tones of the opening betray a sentimentalist rather than a sensationalist (as in Half-Rome), and instead of erring courageously, he prefers the way of compromise avoiding anything of radical, perilous, or even mildly different odour. His is the *via media* become the *via mediocrita*:

> Who can be absolute for either side:
> A middle course is happily open yet.
>   (III, 1379)

He is a fatalist in religion, almost a supporter of natural theology (like Caliban), who can understand the crushing of Pompilia's "flower-like body" as the arbitrary judgment of cause and effect.

Other Half-Rome also uses the Adam-Eve-Eden metaphor that Half-Rome had developed, but here it is used differently with Pietro Comparini as Adam tempted by his wife, Eve-Violante, by means of the apple of their eye, Pompilia. The relationship between Pompilia and Caponsacchi is expanded in the superb light and star imagery which characterizes it throughout the poem. It had been hinted at in Half-Rome's speech where Pompilia is described at Arezzo as "a gleam i' the gloom" (II, 324) and there is at least one mention of the "love-star" (II, 1074) for Pompilia and Caponsacchi. The imagery is combined with the same sense of the timeless or infinite moment which we saw in *By the Fireside*, and the "friendly star" of *Two in the Campagna* for which it is "finite hearts that yearn." The Other Half-Rome goes further in combining his image with another prevalent theme, that of the St. George legend, associated so frequently with Caponsacchi. As is Browning's custom, it is introduced here with only the slightest hint. Pompilia goes to the window to look for the salvation that God will provide,

> And there found Caponsacchi wait as well
> For the precious something at perdition's edge,
> He only was predestinate to save,—
> And if they recognized in a critical flash
> From the zenith, each the other, her need of him,
> His need of . . . say, a woman to perish for
> The regular way o' the world, yet break no vow,
> Do no harm save to himself,—if this were thus?
> How do you say? It were improbable;
> So is the legend of my patron-saint.
> . . . The strange sudden interview
> Blazed as when star and star must needs go close
> Till each hurts each and there is loss in heaven— . . .
> Pompilia and Caponsacchi met, in fine . . .
> And understood each other at first look.
>
> (III, 1042–63)

This is the moment of insight, "the resplendent minute" (III, 1562), but quickly it is gone. Other Half-Rome has hit on the great theme which both Pompilia and Caponsacchi are later to stress, and the Pope to expound theologically. Other Half-Rome sees that the "resplendant minute" when the two meet is also the "critical moment." A choice must be made—for action or for acquiescence. The understanding which illuminates the action of Pompilia and Caponsacchi comes from the merging of their two souls in a love relationship.

Other Half-Rome also asks the pertinent question about truth:

> Now begins
> The tenebrific passage of the tale:
> How hold a light, display the cavern's gorge?
> How, in this phase of the affair, show truth?
>
> (III, 788–9)

Pompilia's purity is the truth, and for him this is the "pure crude fact":

> Anyhow,
> Here be facts, charactery; what they spell
> Determine, and thence pick what sense you may!
>
> (III, 836–8)

Our earlier picture of Guido is reversed, for,

> His facts are lies: his letters are the fact—
> An infiltration flavoured with himself!
>
> (III, 1360)

Fancies about illicit love confound "the midday blaze of truth." Other Half-Rome leaves us in the same position as Half-Rome did. We have not yet come near to the revelatory moment.

Tertium Quid tries to be the detached, analytical critic, judging on the basis of "the established fact" (IV, 42), and coming to a wholly rational, and, of course, "true" decision. But he fails through indecision. *Tertium Quid* criticizes Guido's conduct in words that could well be his own epitaph, for he too

> . . . stands
> Bewildered at the critical minute,—since
> He has the first flash of the fact alone
> To judge from, act with, not the steady lights
> Of after-knowledge . . .
> He'll know in a minute, but till then, he doubts.
>
> (IV, 1182–9)

Tertium Quid does not realize that doubt is a necessary part of man's condition, and after-knowledge is never adequate to correct false action.

He has lost the critical minute in inaction. He did not choose and so he cannot act. This movement in the thought of *Tertium Quid* is the death-motive, a sort of death-in-life that comes from refusing to stand on conviction.

A thick overlay of rumour and fanciful interpretation has prepared us for the advent of the main characters of *The Ring and the Book*. Guido is presented formally as the Count hiding behind the assumed mask of seeming-meekness, fresh from his rack of torture, and so able to excite all our sympathy. From his monologue it becomes clear that the critical moment for him was the whole sequence of events leading up to Christmas Eve when he arrived in Rome. Pompilia is the lure (V, 1400); and the Eden metaphor is used with Violante playing the role of the serpent. In his discussion of truth, irony vies with deceit to have first place, for "the fact's the thing" he bursts out:

> Let me, a man, manfully meet the fact,
> Confront the worst o' the truth, end, and have peace!
>
> (V. 1391)

Guido's own position has shifted many times in the monologues, from putting his case in the hands of the civil law, the Church, natural law, God, his judges, and so on. But it becomes clear that Guido has erred throughout the argument just as he had throughout his life in equating God with nature by lowering him to the letter of the natural law. He has exalted the civil law into the *lex Dei*. Thus it is understandable that he could not fathom the meaning of Christmas when he did not know the real nature of God.

Guido's relation to the Incarnation is revealed in the direct connection with the festival of the Incarnation, Christmas Day. He arrives in Rome intent upon the execution of his revenge, but it is Christmas Eve:

> Festive bells—everywhere the Feast o' the Babe,
> Joy upon earth, peace and good will to man!
>
> (V, 1582)

Irony permeates these lines, as Guido tells how "nine days o' the Birth-Feast did I pause and pray/To enter into no temptation more." The birth of Christ strove to

> . . . quench
> The antagonistic spark of hell and tread
> Satan and all his malice into dust.
>
> (V, 1575)

But Guido has not experienced the revealing and transforming truth, because he can withstand the temptation no longer, and the hesitant doubt turns to determination of will; choice becomes act. The thought, though evil, is carried through into action, and the only light is the dark satanic fire smouldering in his soul:

> On the ninth day, this grew too much for man.
> I started up—"Some end must be!" At once,
> Silence: then, scratching like a death-watch-tick,
> Slowly within my brain was syllabled,
> "One more concession, one decisive way
> And but one, to determine thee the truth,—
> This way, in fine, I whisper in they ear:
> Now doubt, anon decide, thereupon act!"
>
> (V, 1611–18)

The evil that is the truth of Guido is an inversion of truth. He acts, but in a demonic light rather than in a moment of vision. It seems that the Christmas Festival almost drives him to act—it certainly forces him to choose; that he chose wrongly is decisive. The moment of the murder leads to an eternity of repentance.

Guido is the slave of clock-time, the equal moments which make his life mere existence. Pompilia had experienced something more, but her period of waiting for deliverance is a period of clock-time that is mere existence. When Caponsacchi comes, then she begins to live because she starts to see life as it is, filled with beauty, truth, love, and potentiality. The whole poem is a *duration*, as Von Hügel defines the word, "an ever more or less overlapping succession, capable of being concentrated into quasi-simultaneities."[2] Because the poem combines so many concepts of time, it could be regarded itself as a study in Eternal Life. That certainly is one of the aspects in which Browning viewed it.

Caponsacchi, filled with emotion, is unable to control his discourse, and so bursts into the smoke-metaphor used to introduce the three speakers in Book One:

> Have patience! In this sudden smoke from hell,—
> So things disguise themselves,—I cannot see. . . .
>
> (VI, 2)

He cannot see because he is operating only with the feelings, and is at

[2]Von Hügel, *Eternal Life*, 384.

the moment unable to let the brain and soul have their proper place. He, like the others, uses the same themes, but plays a different variation on the same material. He deals with the Garden of Eden theme (VI, 1002) and makes the necessary adaptations. But it is his relation to Pompilia that is the real reason for the book's interest. He cannot forget her because Pompilia is to him "the glory of life, the beauty of the world, the splendour of heaven" (VI, 118). Caponsacchi has not learned to make the proper distinction between the love of earth and the love of heaven, which is not a difference of degree or quality or quantity. The love of earth, as the Pope is to explain, is analogous to the love of heaven in a way that the scholastic theologian calls the analogy of proper proportionality. Caponsacchi is too prone to make the analogy one of simple equivocation. It is valid for him to elaborate the splendour of Pompilia in the theatre-meeting. But for Caponsacchi it is really the turning-point in his life; it is his *anagnorisis*, his moment of epiphany. At this crucial point, while the action moves towards flight (VI, 1076), Caponsacchi's servant introduces the Perseus–Andromeda–St. George legend, "to-morrow is Saint George" (VI, 1111), and Caponsacchi comes to his moment of whiteness:

> When the ecstatic minute must bring birth,
> Began whiteness in the distance, waxed
> Whiter and whiter, near grew and more near,
> Till it was she: there did Pompilia come:
> The white I saw shine through her was her soul's. . . .
>   (VI, 1138–42)

Caponsacchi's moment of whiteness is so intense and concentrated that it completely illuminates his whole horizon; he cannot see anything else. Here is a practical and fully developed treatment of the love-illumination that transforms the love-experience into the moment of Incarnation in the life of the loving soul. Browning has tried to combine some elements of religious love here too, but the full incorporation of spiritual love must wait until the Pope's monologue; there too, full play is given to the artist in the treatment of the Euripides section. Browning is making use of all that he has learned of the relation between time and the suspension of it in the revelatory moment. All the earlier elements of his poetry find their focus and relation in *The Ring and the Book*. Here in Caponsacchi we begin to see how they are gathered together.

Caponsacchi was moved to choose in his relation with Pompilia, and the choosing involved a motivation to act by love. "What Is" led to the choice in "what Knows," and that in turn moved the priest to "what Does." Power and knowledge and love again are intertwined. Caponsacchi, in his moment of revelation, sees that the whiteness of Pompilia is the purity of her soul, and so his action in saving her is the rescuing of sanctity from the designs of evil. He can recognize sanctity by means of the love that he has been living as a priest; he can act to save Pompilia by means of the love that he has for her as a man. Pompilia herself almost seems to be an incarnation of love in a sense similar to Browning's speaking of Sordello as the "incarnation of the people's hope." An encounter with incarnational love involves a response and a radical change. Thus Caponsacchi is now to act wholly in her light as a pale reflection of the light of God. Time has ceased for a moment, and eternity opened on his sight.

At the end of his monologue he has calmed down, and can say that man learns "not only by a comet's rush,/But a rose's birth,—not by the grandeur, God,—/But the comfort, Christ" (VI, 2094). Conversion to the cause of incarnational love is not necessarily by means of a Damascus road flash as in the case of St. Paul; it can also be the hesitant and doubting way of St. Thomas. Pompilia is for Caponsacchi not only the comet, but also the rose—and he has learned to see the bright light of love's truth from both.

Now St. George rescues the maiden Pompilia from the dragon Guido. DeVane has published an article on the theme, "The Virgin and the Dragon,"[3] in which he notes that the Perseus-Andromeda legend was a private myth for Browning (he had an engraved copy of Caravaggio's painting of it above his desk) representing his love for Elizabeth Barrett. In *The Ring and the Book*, Browning adds to this legend the story of St. George from Jacobus de Voraigne's *Legenda Aurea* (we note the significance of the "*Golden*" *Legend*) so that DeVane writes: "Here we see Pompilia–Mrs. Browning–Andromeda rescued from the dragon Guido by Caponsacchi–Browning–Perseus, first; and later when truth or justice is endangered, Pope Innocent, the viceregent of God, is the rescuer." There are, DeVane tells us, at least thirty references to the myth in the books of the poem where favourable judgment is given on Pompilia and Caponsacchi. Nor was Browning

[3] *Yale Review*, September, 1947.

finished with this theme of salvation which he had begun in *Pauline* (and the words apply equally well to Pompilia):

> And she is with me: years roll, I shall change,
> But change can touch her not . . . a thing
> I doubt not, nor fear for, secure some god
> To save will come in thunder from the stars.
> (657–67)

The pattern makes use of the ideas that we might expect in Browning—there is a suspension of the time-sequence, or an elevation of it into a realm *sub specie aeternitatis*, and the method of salvation is an incarnational one. Just two years before Browning's death the same figure is used in the *Parleying with Francis Furini*. All of the symbolic details are there—the figures, the goodness of the flesh (in-carnation), the whole scene in darkness with a single beam of light ("the daystar from on high has visited us"; or the whiteness of the stars; or the light of Pompilia's soul), the colours red, black, and white. However, several more salient points emerge when we go back to Browning's source. In the St. George legend it is not only the dragon which is killed, but later the saint himself. That is why he is regarded as the "Great Martyr" in the sanctorals of the Eastern Church. Western mediaeval St. George plays (and so the account in the *Legenda Aurea*) followed this tradition most scrupulously. But the hero could not be left dead, so he was revived by a doctor of physic. One is left with an essentially tragic action moving from the struggle (*Agon*) to the death (*Pathos*), to the discovery or recognition (*Anagnorisis*), the tearing to pieces (*Sparagmos*), and the final movement to triumph or catastrophe. Browning has made Caponsacchi struggle with himself (and he also has a sort of objective conflict with Guido). Then occur the deaths of the Comparini and Pompilia (also the symbolic death of Caponsacchi in his banishment), the discovery or recognition in the quest for truth on the part of the Pope who is the doctor of metaphysic, restoring justice, life to Caponsacchi, sanctity to Pompilia, and eventually catastrophe to Guido. Throughout this pattern, there is a constant reference to the suspension of time in the moments of illumination or revelation, now on the human love level, and now on the supernatural level of divine love as all of these experiences are related to the Incarnation of Christ in the Pope's monologue. The St. George myth becomes a most powerful means of gathering the elements together under a symbolic guise that is at once intensely personal to the loves of Robert and Elizabeth Browning and also objective because of its wider implications. The myth then becomes even more central to both the themes *and structure* than one at first suspects.

It is with Caponsacchi that the concept of truth in *The Ring and the Book* begins to clear. Perhaps this is what misleads Henry James into saying that he finds the needed centre for his field "in the entrancing consciousness of Caponsacchi . . . ; everything that happens happens most effectively to Caponsacchi's life. . . . So it is *he* contains the whole —unless indeed, after all, the Pope does, the Pope whom I was leaving out as too transcendent for *our* vision."[4] Caponsacchi is devoted to truth, although it is an intensely personal truth—"I need that you should know my truth" (VI, 342). He had been concerned with the fact which "seems to fill the universe with sight and sound" (VI, 64), the fact of Pompilia's death, but this was an emotional, overwrought outburst. He moves further when he accepts Pompilia as "my own fact, my miracle self-authorized and self-explained . . . potency of truth" (VI, 919). He says that a man can become "drunk with truth," and in a sense he has become drunk with the truth of Pompilia who is partly truth to him. He certainly does love her, although he denies it ("as for love,—no!" [VI, 1969]) but he must love her as he loves truth, for she is his revelation of it:

> . . . the revelation of Pompilia. There!
> Such is the final fact I fling you, Sirs,
> To mouth and mumble and misinterpret: there! . . .
> . . . You see the truth—
> I am glad I helped you: she helped me just so.
> (VI, 1865–84)

This, though, is mortal truth, just as this love is mortal love. Caponsacchi would go further, as indeed he does (and as is made even clearer in Pompilia's and the Pope's monologues) to combine the love of man and woman (as seen in *Two in the Campagna* or *By the Fireside*) with the love of God (the other aspect, fuller, richer, in Browning's monologues, like *Saul* or *Abt Vogler*). Caponsacchi is still, it seems, moving towards the harmonious calm which perfect union of these kinds of love (seen in Pompilia) will bring.[5] Nevertheless, he is a priest; his vision of

[4]Henry James, *Quarterly Review*, July, 1912, 75–87.

[5]Professor Hoxie Neale Fairchild has rightly stressed the Incarnation in Browning's thought, but his viewing of love, physical erotic love, as an end in itself, seems to be too narrow a view,

Utopia, contrasting with Guido's earthly paradise at the end of his speech, is of the Heavenly Jerusalem:

> I thirst for truth,
> But shall not drink it till I reach the source . . .
> To have to do with nothing but the true,
> The good, the eternal. . . .   (VI, 2067–90)

The anguish then floods his soul in his pitiful, personal sorrow as he accepts the faintly understood mercy of God:

> O great, just, good God! Miserable me! (VI, 2105)

The climax of these three central books of the poem, after the polished rhetoric of Guido and Caponsacchi's emotional grief, comes in Pompilia's book. Hers is a strange book in the structure. One may legitimately ask how Book VII could be a climax since it moves at a much quieter pace than the previous two books. Yet such a question would be too superficial. An emotional intensity in Pompilia's monologue always lies below the surface of unruffled calm. One feels that here there is a dispassionate death's-door view of the world, the flesh, and God, a view which in the midst of a set of this-worldly experiences reveals an other-worldly attitude. Her voice of one who is "to die to-night" has the somber note of finality in it which is wholly convincing.

Pompilia immediately reveals her love for Gaetano, her son, and almost in the next breath begins her description of the murder. So closely linked are life and death for Pompilia. She draws a number of parallels between the Incarnation and the birth of Gaetano, as Guido had also done, though in a different context:

> That fancy which began so faint at first,
> That thrill of dawn's suffusion through my dark,
> Which I perceive was promise of my child,
> The light his unborn face sent long before,—
> God's way of breaking the good news to flesh.
>   (VII, 621–5)

---

missing the point that Browning's characteristic mode of imparting truth is analogical discourse: The great thing, of course, was love— . . . ; for Browning the best love is sexual love regarded as a sort of Caponsacchi-Pompilia or Perseus-Andromeda or Robert-Elizabeth incarnation. It is very important for Browning that the Word should be made *flesh*—so important that in the erotic union of human and divine the fleshification of spirit is sometimes more obvious than the spiritualization of flesh. (*Religious Trends in English Poetry*, IV, 147.)

The birth of her son is regarded in terms of God's creative act in each child, and it is expressed through the customary symbol of the Incarnation of the Good News, another reference that Browning tucked into the allusion. Caponsacchi is spoken of in the same terms used for Gaetano. He is the incarnation of Pompilia's hope and just as she had shone out clear purity from her soul to his, so Caponsacchi flashes to her:

> The glory of his nature, I had thought,
> Shot itself out in white light, blazed the truth
> Through every atom of his act with me. . . .
> (VII, 921–3)

His is a "lustrous and pelucid soul," and it lights her way no less than her soul leads his. Pompilia finds only truth and love in her "soldier-saint." But she has found a greater love than an earthly one, and, unlike Caponsacchi, she is about to drink that love at its source. All of her life has been lived in a close relationship with God; now at the end of it she sees everything, all of her actions and inactions, with great objective clarity and vision. Her anguish, pain, suffering, and even grief have faded into the devouring past; the future is life and love and truth. Evil too is seen to be transitory as all things are resolved into the good, if not with a joyful hope, at least with a prayerful optimism.

Pompilia regards Caponsacchi as her St. George and again there is a converging of symbols about these figures. She regards herself as light, her vision as a circle, a ring of truth:

> I wish nor want
> One point o' the circle plainer, where I stand
> Traced round about with white to front the world.
> (VII, 1644–6)

To her Caponsacchi is the star of light in her "throe of the dusk" (VII, 1406). He is her star leading her to the place where her dayspring, Gaetano, will be born.[6] They follow the star in each other much as the Magi followed Bethlehem's star, and they carry the same elements with them—the gold of truth and love, the incense of holiness, and the myrrh of death. She, thinking of her child, finds it easy to associate herself with the Blessed Virgin:

> So did the star rise, soon to lead my step,
> Lead on, nor pause before it should stand still

[6]See Smith, *Browning's Star Imagery*, where Caponsacchi is interpreted as a leading star guiding Pompilia; with the Pope the star becomes the symbol of universal truth.

> Above the House o' the Babe,—my babe to be . . .
> No pause i' the leading and the light! I know,
> Next night there was a cloud came, and not he:
> But I prayed through the darkness till it broke
> And let him shine. The second night, he came.
>
> (VII, 1448–61)

Pompilia awaited the illumination that would come to announce her salvation. She had to act in the flight with Caponsacchi—she had to risk all to attain her freedom. The giving of everything characterized the total gift, and so Pompilia's giving of everything in her choice is analogous to the action of God's gift in Incarnation. Browning points out the parallel with the Incarnation in terms of the flight into Egypt (IX, 74, 122) where all was risked and all was attained. Pompilia, in the moment of critical choice, decides on the basis of love, the surest foundation of truth. That love, which she could not find in her marriage, she finds in God and in his servant, Caponsacchi, who leads her to incarnation. Caponsacchi advised, "'Leave God the way,'" thereby turning Pompilia to a complete reliance in a just God's ways to men, so that she sees Caponsacchi to be the revealer of truth, the soldier, the saint, and even something of truth itself as all of the themes (after her penetrating remark on Guido, "hate was thus the truth of him" [VII 1727]) unite in the concluding coda of her monologue:

> The day-star stopped its task that makes night morn!
> O lover of my life, O soldier-saint,
> No work begun shall ever pause for death!
> Love will be helpful to me more and more
> I' the coming course, the new path I must tread— . . .
> Meantime hold hard by truth and his great soul,
> Do out the duty! Through such souls alone
> God stooping shows sufficient of His light
> For us i' the dark to rise by. And I rise.
>
> (VII, 1785–9, 1843–6)

Pompilia's analysis of her incarnational experience has been somewhat more profound than Caponsacchi's, partly because her monologue is delivered when the exigencies of time and space have faded before the greater realities of eternity and heaven. But there still needs to be a philosophical and theological justification for the events and the opinions which the characters experienced and hold.

Browning interjects two monologues from the courts "to sober us" and to "teach our common sense its helplessness" (I, 1106). The lawyers provide a time-lag in the action to allow Pompilia to die, and the Pope to begin to develop his meditation on the facts and the truth. Relief comes after the hagiographic study of Pompilia with the interlude of burlesque from the lawyers. Archangelis and Bottinius bring again to the fore many of the recurrent themes—society and the mob, mercy and justice, fact and fancy, nature and law, and so on. We also hear again (from Bottinius) about Pompilia as Eve before the Fall, and the St. George legend. Neither lawyer is in a position to let love interfere with his analysis of the case, and so both remain removed from any real relationship with the Incarnation. Consequently their conclusions remain solely on the natural level, and are bound by temporal considerations of family, stomach, and public opinion; they have nothing of eternity or grace. The position that has been reached by Browning is succinctly put, and leads directly on into Book X:

> . . . but the Proof, . . . the result,
> O' the Trial, and the style of punishment, . . .
> All is tentative, till the sentence come.
>
> (IX, 1535-9)

3. THE POPE

> Cried the Pope's great self,—Innocent by name
> And nature too, and eighty-six years old,
> Antonio Pignatelli of Naples, Pope
> Who had trod many lands, known many deeds,
> Probed many hearts, beginning with his own,
> And now was far in readiness for God,— . . .
> —He cried of a sudden, this great good old Pope,
> When they appealed in last resort to him,
> "I have mastered the whole matter: I nothing doubt."
>
> (I, 300-28)

"The Pope, that good Twelfth Innocent" (I, 821) presents "the ultimate judgment save yours" (I, 1220). He is the most complex and subtle of Browning's characters in the poem, and perhaps the greatest that he ever created, even including Sordello and Paracelsus. The Pope speaks what could almost be regarded as Browning's own Apology, and in the poem acts as a *deus ex machina*. In Book I Browning had outlined the circumstances of the monologue as the Pope, reading aloud, "lets flow his own thoughts forth likewise aloud" (I, 1258). To bear on the case the Pope brings the power of his office, the knowledge of his years, and the love of his God. The venerable Pope has studied for many years the rules and exercises of both holy living and holy dying, so that his meditated attitude to life gives his book its objectivity. Innocent's vision seems to be made even clearer (as we also saw in Pompilia's insight) by the approach of his death; again we are reminded of his ancestor among the Apostles, St. John, dying in the desert, and stressing the same doctrines.

Since all of the characters are weighed in the balances of the Pope, there are many explicit comparisons with earlier opinions expressed either by the character himself, or by his advocate. Thus Guido is set against the view expressed by the spectre, Antonio Pignatelli, his former self, "man is born nowise to content himself, but please God" (X, 435). But Guido had failed to live up to his obligation, and failed "most in the last deliberate act" (X, 522). Guido chose wrongly in rejecting the sure sounding of the Word of Truth and so he loses all. The Pope ironically affirms, "I nothing doubt" (I, 328), and as elsewhere in Browning, this kind of certainty spells death, here the death of Guido and his accomplices. Pompilia is vindicated for she is "perfect in whiteness." In a noble paragraph the "poor old Pope" pays tribute to her as a pure soul like Dante's Beatrice (X, 1004). She did not have great intellectual powers, but she had what was much greater, "purity and patience":

> My flower,
> My rose, I gather for the breast of God
> This I praise most in thee, where all I praise,
> That having been obedient to the end
> According to the light allotted, law
> Prescribed thy life. . . . Go past me
> And get thy praise,—and be not far to seek
> Presently when I follow if I may! (X, 1046-94)

Caponsacchi is described in familiar terms as the "warrior priest," the champion of virtue, the St. George, the bright star of salvation. But he is also the "irregular noble scapegrace." The Pope sees wider than the moment of revelation which Caponsacchi had glimpsed, because he can place the moment of revelation in a context of redeemed history where life is made meaningful just by that moment of revelation. In this context man has to choose the good and reject the evil; his striving to ascertain each is to use all of his powers, and so he cannot afford to rely on his emotions alone for the interpretation of the revelation:

> Never again elude the choice of tints!
> White shall not neutralize the black, nor good
> Compensate bad in man, absolve him so:
> Life's business being just the terrible choice.
>
> (X, 1235–8)

Thus the deliberation over the *dramatis personae* ends, and the sagacious Pope returns to the mood of reflective contemplation as he begins the theological disquisition. Here is the intellectual centre of the poem, for in it lies a key to the whole meaning. The judgments are simply the practical application of his vision of life.

The Pope begins by facing squarely the terrifying possibility that he may have erred. His examination of his predecessors on the Chair of Peter only shows him that doubt has its very real role to play, since doubt is the means by which man is tried. "Why should I doubt?" (X, 910), he asks, but then "the gaunt gray nightmare in the farthest smoke" clouds over the light of certainty. He had known the truth, but that enables man to choose correctly; it does not remove doubt or the necessity of choice:

> Yet my poor spark had for its source, the sun;
> Thither I sent the great looks which compel
> Light from its fount: all that I do and am
> Comes from the truth, or seen or else surmised,
> Remembered or divined, as mere man may:
> I know just so, nor otherwise . . .
> All to the very end is trial in life:
> At this stage is the trial of my soul
> Danger to face or danger to refuse?
> Shall I dare try the doubt now, or not dare?
>
> (X, 1285–1307)

He must trust in the infinite wisdom of God, and so he begins to pray as he moves with the light that he has, the light of the Incarnation:

> In God's name! Once more on this earth of God's,
> While twilight lasts and time wherein to work,
> I take His staff with my uncertain hand, . . .
> The Pope for Christ.   (X, 163–9)

His winter's meditation in the winter of his age leads him to consider that "truth, nowhere, lies yet everywhere in these," the figures of fact, the accounts of the trial. But these trivial facts only show to Innocent that man's speech is presumption, and only has worth in the full truth of the authoritative Word that God spoke in his Son. Man says that he knows truth, but he really knows only two things, "that I am I, as He is He" (X, 381), as Browning demonstrated in *La Saisiaz*. Words are an inadequate expression of truth, yet they are redeemed by the one perfect word, the *Logos*:

> Therefore these filthy rags of speech, this coil
> Of statement, comment, query and response,
> Tatters all too contaminate for use,
> Have no renewing: He, the Truth, is, too,
> The Word. (X, 373-7)

St. John's Gospel, so significant for Browning, uses the doctrine of the *Logos* in chapter 1 to make the valuable connection between God and Man in the God-man, the Word of God. Such a Word is the way, the truth, and the life, and is "spoken" by God in flesh. Because Christ is the Word of God, all other words are really analogous to God's spoken action in his *fiat* of creation and redemption. Christ as Word, and the Bible as the recorded action of God, the "Word" in another written sense, stamp authenticity on human speech, because in that God's word is final, so all imitations or analogues of that word partake of the nature of that finality as far as their nature will allow. It is on this level of analogy that the poetic activity is seen in its most clear light. Poetry can be a means of communicating divine and ultimate truth in an oblique manner simply because it partakes of the finality of the creative and saving acts of God through the use of the analogous word. Christ, by his nature as *Logos*, is ultimately associated with human language, and so he also shares with the poet the obligation of revealing truth through the mediate word. The cogency of this part of the monologue of Innocent comes from the fact that it is the basis of Innocent's estimation of the trial. Just as the analysis of the Three Souls and the place in this scheme of the Incarnation is essential to the thought of *A Death in the Desert*, just as the Incarnation connects art to life in the monologues on painting and music, and just as the Incarnation provides the analogue for human love in the love lyrics, so here again it is the central and controlling doctrine. The Pope's meditation is rooted and grounded in the source of love, God's Son, and his application of the theological framework to the present situation has to be explained to Browning's readers, if they are to move with the Pope to accept the conclusion. To regard the meditation as a digression is a triumph of superficiality.

The Pope applies the *Logos* doctrine not only to the murder trial, but

also to himself as he alone of the characters examines his own motivation as of one who is "only man," but a man whose "poor spark had
for its source, the sun" (X, 1285). A number of earlier themes are
brought together at this point in the Pope's interior monologue. Like
the Sun-treader of *Pauline*, the Pope believes "in God and truth and
love" and he is also aware of the two "knows" which will characterize
a later poem, the knowledge of his own existence, and the knowledge
of the existence of God in *La Saisiaz*. The objective and the subjective
natures and kinds of poet, which Browning had examined in the
Essay on Shelley, and in *Paracelsus* and *Sordello*, come to prime importance in the balancing of the two elements in the Pope's monologue.
The creative minds of the poet, of the Pope, and of Browning himself
are also concerned, as usual, with the moral implications of life, and
these are brought to bear on the Pope's meditation as part of the subjective reaching beyond itself to wider and more objective considerations. Again the familiar analysis of experience in terms of power,
goodness, and love is developed by Browning (X, 1336 ff.). But while
in *A Death in the Desert* the doctrine appeard as a gloss in parentheses, in
the Pope's monologue it is introduced with the sure poetic sense that
both the doctrine and its expression are integral to the monologue and
the character of its speaker. Man's instinctive goodness, man's capability
of loving, is corrupted by pride. But by means of suffering, sorrow, and
pain, something of the pride may be eliminated. An act of self-sacrifice,
itself the denial of pride, then becomes possible in a new creative, and
moral universe:

> I can believe this dread machinery
> Of sin and sorrow, would confound me else,
> Devised—all pain, at most expenditure
> Of pain by Who devised pain—to evolve,
> By new machinery in counterpart,
> The moral qualities of man—how else?—
> To make him love in turn and be beloved,
> Creative and self-sacrificing too,
> And thus eventually God-like. . . .
>
> (X, 1375-83)

Here at last is the explanation of the place of Pompilia's anguish and
Guido's evil.

Evil in *The Ring and the Book* (and that poetic world for Browning
represents life) is temporal and fleeting. It serves only to illustrate the

power and the love of God, because evil is constantly transformed by God into good. When it is turned into moral necessity, it has its part to play in God's scheme for the regeneration of man. But the choice of evil or good is not a necessary compulsion; it is a voluntary choice in time and must be motivated by love if it is to be God-like. Pigou comments that "time is unreal from God's point of view so that pain and evil, being events in Time, can only be real for men."[7] To Browning God is outside time and space,[8] but man can experience the eternal in life as well as temporal experiences in spatial reality. Eternity broke through time in the Incarnation, but both the Pope and St. John dread the universal prick of light through the flesh grown thin. This is the reality that human kind cannot bear readily. Man knows that perfection is God's secret, and it exists outside and independent of time, but man must struggle for the perfection that he knows in the Moment which is in time. The struggle to know the Moment is often the cause of pain and anguish, and the struggle is against the evil which constantly threatens to overcome the meaning of the moment. It is a final battle against this evil that the Pope is suffering now, thoroughly conscious that the battle has already been won in time by the Incarnation; it remains for him to relate the Incarnation to the present situation. The activity of the judge (or any other role of the Pope, like poet, prophet, or king) is one of self-sacrifice to carry out the incarnational experience in his own flesh. Then love and truth come full into play in a dramatic moment of recreation. That is a moment of revelation, when "God's gloved hand" shows something of eternity to the world. To the Pope,

> Life is probation and the earth no goal
> But starting-point of man; compel him strive. . . .
> (X, 1436-7)

Like Tennyson's Ulysses, man must strive, and find meaning for existence in action; that is the lesson which the Pope learned from his St. Thomas, that God is pure act:[9]

> A thing existent only while it acts,
> Does as designed, else a nonentity. . . .
> (X, 1501-2)

[7]*Browning as a Religious Teacher*, 139.
[8]Robert Browning, *Letters*, ed. Hood, October 11, 1881.
[9]To St. Thomas, the *actus purus* of God is simply to be; that is what God is when he is what he is. *Quis est Deus? Esse est subsistens.*

Pompilia acted, and so did Caponsacchi. In their love through suffering they advanced in the way of holiness, and were strengthened in their journey towards the day-spring. It is in a similar light that the Pope must redeem the time by the love-motivated action.

The glorious answer to the Euripides passage presents the ultimate utopia of *The Ring and the Book*, the *civitas Dei*, the new age, which will be the testing ground of man's faith. Man may fail; what is more important is that God will not. As a phantom from the past, Euripides haunts the Pope's imagination, giving voice to the Pope's own thoughts. How dare he not judge those "who miss the plain way in the blaze of noon," who have the benefit of a full revelation of love in the Incarnation, but ignore it? Euripides had incarnated all he knew into his creative activity by adopting "virtue as my rule of life" and loving for love's sake. If life could be lived then at the zenith in "a tenebrific time," what can be possible in "the sunrise now"? Slowly, slowly, the Pope begins to formulate his crucial answer. But the present is not wholly adequate to bear the weight of his introspection. The Pope exercises his role of prophet in looking into the heart of the new age as he stands Moses-like above the New Israel of the Church. We cannot doubt that Browning is also speaking as the poet-seer of the nineteenth century:

> . . . what whispers me of times to come?
> What if it be the mission of that age
> My death will usher into life, to shake
> This torpor of assurance from our creed,
> Re-introduce the doubt discarded, bring
> That formidable danger back, we drove
> Long ago to the distance and the dark?
>
> (X, 1851–7)

Then will man still be able to avoid anthropomorphism in his concept of divinity, the necessary correction to the tendency seen in *Saul*:

> Correct the portrait by the living face,
> Man's God, by God's God in the mind of man.
>
> (X, 1873–4)

The Pope is at the end of his life ("Do not we end, the century and I?" X, 1903), but he has his last choice to make and act to perform:

> Still, I stand here, not off the stage though close
> On the exit: and my last act, as my first,

> I owe the scene, and Him who armed me thus
> With Paul's sword as with Peter's key. I smite
> With my whole strength once more, ere end my part,
> Ending, so far as man may, this offence.
> (X, 1955–60)

He asks the same question asked by Guido, but with true earnestness, "*Quis pro Domino?*" (X, 2100), and the Pope can answer with determination of will, now that doubt has solidified his faith, "I, who write. . . ."

In a final swift movement the Pope brilliantly uses satire and irony to deal with the arguers and their arguments, culminating in his verdict on Guido: "they die to-morrow. . . . Let there be prayer incessant for the five." Still Guido is not lost. The justic of God, unlike that of the Pope, is perfect, and it is into the hands of that justice that the Pope commits Guido. There God's justice will combine with his wisdom and mercy, so that Guido will be remade. The monologue ends with a symbolic description of a landscape, as so many of Browning's poems do:

> I stood at Naples once, a night so dark
> I could have scarce conjectured there was earth
> Anywhere, sky or sea or world at all:
> But the night's black was burst through by a blaze—
> Thunder struck blow on blow, earth groaned and bore,
> Through her whole length of mountain visible:
> There lay the city thick and plain with spires,
> And, like a ghost disshrouded, white the sea.
> (X, 2119–26)

The symbols of the vision are typically Browning's: thunder, lightning flashing to reveal the knowledge of man erected into cities, and the power of God in the white strength of the sea. The moment is apocalyptic and it reminds us of other moments in the Browning canon, at the end of *Saul*, or *An Epistle*; in blinding clarity the world of nature mirrors the revelation of the world of grace. The Pope connects the moment of revelation with the plight of Guido:

> So may the truth be flashed out by one blow,
> And Guido see, one instant, and be saved.
> (X, 2127–8)

God is not the destroying angel, but the redeeming Saviour, and

Browning sees his activity not as punishing evil, but as remaking those whom evil has destroyed. Innocent asks his final question of his soul and of God:

> Enough, for I may die this very night:
> And how should I dare die, this man let live?
>
> (X, 2133–4)

The Pope's act, like every act of every man, is hovering on the brink of death. Death will give the final stamp of meaning to each life, and the Pope's action, *"pro Domino,"* casts its light over the whole poem, giving it its meaning, to Browning and to us.

4. THE SUMMATION

The narrative, except for the execution, is over with the end of the Pope's monologue, but we have one more look at Guido to see a different aspect of his character from that previously seen. The study of evil has rather obvious parallels with the study of virtue seen in Pompilia. Guido, like the Pope and Pompilia, is at the point of death, and the clarity of his vision brings with it a hysterical note as the hate which Pompilia said was the truth of him is claimed as his own; "hate of all things in, under, and above earth" (XI, 1798). Guido lapses into a mechanistic pessimism, the antithesis to the faith of the Pope and Pompilia:

> Unbelief still might work the wires and move
> Man, the machine, to play a faithful part.
>
> (XI, 612–13)

Power and intelligence, what the Pope saw in nature, cannot save where there is no love, and so Guido is crushed by the natural law, as his own code demands. He had demanded complete success, and yet his own life is founded on an incomplete view of existence:

> Inscribe all human effort with one word,
> Artistry's haunting curse, the Incomplete!
> Being incomplete, my act escaped success.
>
> (XI, 1560–2)

Guido has missed the only completion known in this life, the completion of the Moment of Incarnation, and so he has no place for the striving for meaning in the doctrine of the Imperfect. His life, since it has failed in its attempt to achieve perfection, is worthless in his own eyes, as Guido cries, "What's the worth of life?" (XI, 2331). The answer comes with a dreadful final irony in Guido's last agonized cry. The death choice of the Pope acting for God was eternal; Guido desires the prolongation of mere temporality; he fears the eternal. He denied it a place in this life, and closed his eyes to its light. Now, on the brink of destruction, when the critical moment is lost,

> Life is all!
> I was just stark mad,—let the madman live . . .
> Don't open! Hold me from them! I am yours,
> I am the Granduke's—no, I am the Pope's!
> Abate,—Cardinal,—Christ,—Maria,—God, . . .
> Pompilia, will you let them murder me?
>
> (XI, 2421–7)

The chit-chat of Book XII balances that of Book I, and we are back again to the house of rumour, of Rome, and Half-Rome and Tertium Quid. Into this atmosphere Browning walks, speaking *in propria persona*, once more tossing the *Old Yellow Book* into the air with his "Ring that's all but round and done" (XII, 238). Finally, it is given to Fra Celestino to draw together the final threads of the poem in his sermon. Truth is with God:

> And, since truth seems reserved for heaven not earth,
> Plagued here by earth's prerogative of lies,
> Should learn to love and long for what, one day
> Approved by life's probation, he may speak.
>
> (XII, 606–9)

Fra Celestino knows that there are other channels of joy in this world, but he has chosen to drink life at its source, as the Pope had done. The other channels are those which Browning constantly has been examining in his poetry:

> For many a doubt will fain perturb my choice—
> Many a dream of life spent otherwise—
> How human love, in varied shapes, might work
> As glory, or as rapture, or as grace:
> How conversancy with the books that teach,
> The arts that help,—how, to grow good and great,
> Rather than simply good, and bring thereby
> Goodness to breathe and live, nor, born i' the brain,

Die there,—how these and many another gift
Of life are precious though abjured by me.

(XII, 625–34)

The sermon of Fra Celestino, like the monologue of the Pope, moves beyond itself to colour the whole poem with its doctrine. In the gold of the book, in the revelation of God, there is some glimpse, in a moment of vision, or of creative action (as in the creative act of the poet), of that truth which flashes in the darkness. At this moment words are both meaningless and useless. They express the *Logos*, which cannot be expressed, yet which must always be proclaimed as the source and end of art and life, so that men can both accept and use it:

. . . it is the glory and good of Art,
That Art remains the one way possible
Of speaking truth, to mouths like mine at least.

(XII, 842–4)

. . . —Art may tell a truth
Obliquely, do the thing shall breed the thought,
Nor wrong the thought, missing the mediate word.
So may you paint your picture, twice show truth,
Beyond mere imagery on the wall,—
So, note by note, bring music from your mind,
Deeper than ever e'en Beethoven dived,—
So write a book shall mean beyond the facts,
Suffice the eye and save the soul beside.

(XII, 859–67)

It is in these lines that we have spelled out the intimate connection that Browning perceived among the different artistic disciplines. Painting, music, sculpture, poetry have this in common:—they are art-forms which tell a truth obliquely, and do not wrong the thought by missing the mediate word. The mediate Word, the Mediator, is the ultimate truth which art can hope to express, since it is the centre of truth itself. That is why Browning can speak of art as saving the soul; it can do that only because the artistic activity is capable of religious use, and the example of the religious revelation in the Incarnation is the archetype of all creative and redemptive activity.

Browning's ring is as finished as it can be; his posy "linking our England to his Italy" is gracefully concluded with its ascription to his "Lyric Love," both the Muse of Poetry, and the cherished memory of

Elizabeth, so that again in the presentation of the poetic symbol of perfection (the posy) Browning is involving a number of areas of experience (romantic love, poetry, art, religion, the same continuing group of interests). We still ask "What is truth?", and now the "ultimate question" is ours indeed.

The questions which Browning has always asked himself are metaphysical questions. Metaphysics is not concerned with problems which have to be solved, but with mysteries which are (always inadequately) to be described. Austin Farrer in the Bampton Lectures for 1948, *The Glass of Vision*, is much concerned over these matters. He argues that science deals with problems to which there are right answers. Science cultivates a healthy respect for fact; religion is based on a respect for Being. The metaphysician, or the poet, is faced with a mystery, not a series of relations, however complex, and he must try to make something of it. Since the human mind understands in the act of discourse and not by simple intuition, to understand will be to describe. The metaphysician seeks to understand his mysteries in seeking to describe them. However, each of the mysteries that has to be described is unique, and how can one describe the unique? The metaphysician uses analogy, "only another name for sober and appropriate images."[10] Browning's ring and book are such analogies, and Browning is seeking to understand the metaphysical mystery of truth by seeking to describe the ring and the book. He is using what he himself called the "mediate word" to come to terms with the ultimate Word. Browning has always expressed his thought in certain dominant images, and these set forth the supernatural mystery which is the heart of the New Testament. Because the spiritual instruction of the New Testament is related in the most intimate way possible to the great images that are set forth there, that spiritual teaching becomes revealed truth. Man cannot conceive except in images; and these images (for Browning, "Art," as in the closing lines of the poem) must be divinely given to him if he is to know a supernatural divine act. As Farrer says:

Christ clothed himself in the archetypal images, and then began to do and to suffer. The images were further transformed by what Christ suffered and did when he had put them on; they were transformed also by their all being combined in his one person [like Browning's use of this combination in the prophet-priest-king theme]. . . . The images are supernaturally formed, and supernaturally made intelligible to faith.

[10] *The Glass of Vision*, 71.

Faith discerns not the images, but what the images signify; and yet we cannot discern it except *through* the images.[11]

Browning's quest leads him to truth through the images of the characters, and other personal symbols, like the ring, the book, stars, fire, the saint, and so on. The poet is moving an incantation of images under a control. The movement takes place in time, but the incantation speaks of eternity. The control, for Browning, is the Incarnation.

[11]*Ibid.*, 108–10.

VI

UNITY RE-EXAMINED:
THE LAST POEMS

I prefer to look for the highest attainment, not
simply the high,—and, seeing it, I hold by it   (*An Essay on Shelley*).

THE PATTERN OF Browning's writing in the last twenty-two years after
the publication of *The Ring and the Book* until his death in 1889, with
the notable exception of the Greek poetry, was a continuation of the
themes which had been his concern in the early and middle periods of
his life. Again and again the same interests emerge—a fascination with
the grotesque in personal psychology; an examination of the Renaissance; the themes of poetry, religion, art, and love—all separate, and
all intertwined. Delight in out-of-the-way subject matter appears in
Ferishtah's Fancies (1884), but for all of the eastern décor, we note that
the ideas are the same—reworkings of old problems to which Browning
returned until his death.

With the completion of *The Ring and the Book* Browning had offered
his most profound examination of faith and doubt, truth and fancy,
time and Incarnation, an examination towards which all of the earlier
poetry had been pointing with a certain hand. In the years afterwards,
Browning merely looks again at some aspects of the old concerns. He
had made his contribution, and now he had simply to try the vantage
point of a new perspective. Except in the remarkable *Parleyings* (1887)
and some other shorter poems like *La Saisiaz* (1877), the poetic fire
seemed to burn with less intensity, even though it flamed as brightly as
before. Something seemed to be gone from Browning and those who
are interested in psychological motivation for poetry could no doubt

find the loss in the death of Elizabeth. *The Ring and the Book* was the great monument to her memory, and thereafter the single effect was somewhat marred by elaboration.[1] It will complete our purposes to see some of the lines of this elaboration, until it too reaches its termination in *Asolando*.

The interplay of fact and fancy which had comprised much of the interest in *The Ring and the Book* is picked up again in *Fifine at the Fair*. Now it too is wedded to the interest of love, even in the face of death. But death is not to be annihilation, because something will survive the value-stamp that death puts upon life; "Love is all, and Death is naught!" (last line of the *Epilogue*). What has been called optimism in Browning is apparent all through these later poems, and the note of triumph from the end of *Fifine* echoes on into the *Prologue* to *Pacchiarotto*:

> Hold on, hope hard in the subtle thing
> That's spirit. . . .

This hope is not a merely secular form of optimism, but is instead a religious attitude of mind, one of the theological virtues. When it is combined with faith and love, we have a complete picture of Browning's attitude to life, but to call anything in Browning complete is to state a paradox. Hope is not to be cherished alone in a vacuum, but is to be put to work in the world, in each man's life. He had learned from the Incarnation that time has been redeemed, but each man has to strive to make the Incarnation redeem his own time; man is to co-operate with God in the transformation of Babylon into Jerusalem:

> Man's work is to labour and leaven—
> As best he may—earth here with heaven;
> 'Tis work for work's sake he is needing:

[1]Similar patternings have been noticed in the works of many of the great artists in different media. The artist begins with a period of apprenticeship in which he follows closely the style and subject matter of his master. Then follows a period of increasing maturity until the great works of his career are produced. Thereafter comes an elaboration of technique, and greater attention to the technical restrictions or possibilities of the medium he is using. Critics have grown tired in pointing out that pattern in Shakespeare, and it has also been noticed in the paintings of Michael-angelo—from the preliminary studies through to the masterpiece on the Sistine ceiling, and finally ending in the late Vision of Judgment and last sculpture. In Bach we find first a following of Buxtehude and Vivaldi, then the enormous output of the St. Thomas days—the cantatas, Mass in B minor, and the Passions—and finally the complex tonalities and structurings of the last fugues. In Mozart too we move from the primness of early Italian imitations to the last quartets and the Requiem; so also in Beethoven, and many other artists, a similar scheme may be seen.

> Let him work on and on as if speeding
> Work's end, but not dream of succeeding!
> Because if success were intended,
> Why, heaven would begin ere earth ended.
>
> *Pacchiarotto*, xxi

These lines illustrate one more examination of the doctrine of the Imperfect, here seen in its application to life through painting, just as in the earlier Renaissance monologues.

Browning's many-years' study of the problems of belief bore unlooked-for fruit in his attitude to the death of Miss Egerton-Smith. Her sudden death brought again into Browning's mind the problem of the evil in the world. The problem was a personal one to him both because of his sense of bereavement, and also because of his capacity as a poet. Again he has supplied the personal answer which is valid to him in providing life with a coherent scheme. The poet is speaking *in propria persona* in *La Saisiaz*, and so it is natural that his mind, musing in careful pattern over the matter at hand, should return again to earlier themes as he echoes all of the breadth and depth of his poetry from *Pauline* and *Paracelsus* to the present moment: "Goodness, wisdom, power, all bounded, each a human attribute!" To examine the problem, Browning uses the dialogue form (much like that in Tennyson's *The Two Voices*) as Fancy and Reason come to accept the necessary existence of God and the Soul; then the argument moves on:

> God is, and the soul is, and, as certain, after death shall be.
> Put this third to use in life, the time for using fact!
>
> (408–9)

Knowledge, for Browning, must here follow its accustomed path—to the use of knowledge in living. Knowledge is a means of discerning the good and evil in the world, and so is the determining factor in matters of choice. But the actual choice of action remains the really decisive human action. Hope itself, whether in life or in an after life, is a mode of knowledge, and so has also to be used, like all of the theological virtues. Certainty in the knowledge of God does not destroy the reality of human doubt about the place of God who acted in creation. It requires faith and hope to know what God has done in creation, and above all in re-creation through the Incarnation of himself as the Christ. The personal soul is also a matter of certainty, but the soul must choose whether God or mammon will be served, and so again faith and hope, motivated by love, will determine the choice. Knowledge of God and knowledge of the soul remain as two rather isolated pieces of a total knowledge which is known wholly only to God. Browning again is left amazed before the immensity of the divine attributes:

> . . . Least part this: then what the whole?

Browning is conscious throughout this poem of his own personal loss in the death of Miss Egerton-Smith, and that loss brings to his mind his other great loss, still strong in his soul, the death of Elizabeth. It is in the context of these two losses that he can call his Beatrice to his poetic aid as he uses Dante's device in examining the problem:

> . . . I take upon my lips
> Phrase the solemn Tuscan fashioned, and declare the soul's eclipse
> Not the soul's extinction? take his "I believe and I declare—
> Certain am I—from this life I pass into a better, there
> Where that lady lives of whom enamoured was my soul"—where this
> Other lady, my companion dear and true, she also is.
>
> (211-16)

The Beatrice-Elizabeth image acts as a kind of poetic inspiration in the poem, never far below the emotional surface. Love is still the greatest of the virtues, and Browning still lives and writes by its light.[2]

Doubt and faith come to the forefront again in *Jocoseria* (1883), especially in the poem *Jochanan Hakkadosh*. Once more we have a treatment of the place of fleeting love in the cherished memory as time threatens to devour even the moment of revelation in the poem *Never the Time and the Place*. *Ferishtah's Fancies*, published the year after *Jocoseria* in 1884, continues some of the thoughts suggested there. We find the same interest in the life of the Arab as illustrative of life in general. Added personal point is given to the poems by the editorial stanzas printed at the end of each of the poems in the collection. In *A Pillar at Sebzevah* Browning writes on themes which had interested him in *A Death in the Desert* and *An Epistle*:

> ". . . All I seem to know
> Is—I know nothing save that love I can

[2]Cf. Duckworth, *Browning, Background and Conflict* (206-7): ". . . Interpreted in the language of logic, this seeing of the white light of ultimate truth amounts to a co-ordination, a harmonization of the poet's experience—it is the attainment of that unity which the mystic assigns as the essential character of the Supreme Being."

> Boundlessly, endlessly—knowledge means
> Ever-renewed assurance by defeat
> That victory is somehow still to reach,
> But love is victory, the prize itself:
> Love—trust to! . . ." (8–14)

Love is the best and highest mode of knowledge, and it also preserves the value which Browning puts upon the doctrine of the Imperfect since knowledge gained through love, like love, is boundless:

> Were knowledge all thy faculty, then God
> Must be ignored: love gains him by first leap.
> Frankly accept the creatureship: ask good
> To love for: press bold to the tether's end
> Allotted to this life's intelligence!
>
> (132–6)

Choice in Browning has taken the form of striving after the choice to act has been made. *A Bean Stripe* deals again with the knowledge of selfhood and Godhood that were discussed in *La Saisiaz*, but Browning moves closer to the particular application of selfhood in the Incarnation in the later poem:

> Even so
> I needs must blend the quality of man
> With quality of God, and so assist
> Mere human sight to understand my Life,
> What is, what should be,—understand thereby
> Wherefore I hate the first and love the last. . . .
>
> (351–6)

The *Epilogue* to *Ferishtah's Fancies* uses the familiar symbols to express the familiar ideas, the iridescent moon, the "famous ones of old," the meaningful striving as in a battle, and the halo or prize at the end of it all, "Love, thine arms."

The *Parleyings With Certain People of Importance in Their Day* (1887) is Browning's last great attempt at a major poem, and it too, like the other most significant poems of the later years, was called forth by the loss of one dear to Browning, here Milsand. In one final synthetic activity, Browning strives to hold poetic conversations and disputations with men who symbolize abiding interests in his poetic career. Mandeville is the philosopher, Bartoli the historian, Smart the poet, Dodington the politician, Furini and Lairesse the painters, and Avison the musician.

All present problems in psychological interpretation, and through them all runs the problem of poetic communication. How is art, in whatever form, whether religion, philosophy, music, painting, or love, to comment in a meaningful way on life? The *Parleyings* are Browning's last treatment in a systematic way of the problem of the Incarnation, summing up the various ways that Browning has seen the mystery:

> Man, with the narrow mind, must cram inside
> His finite God's infinitude,—earth's vault
> He bids comprise the heavenly far and wide,
> Since Man may claim a right to understand
> What passes understanding.
> (*With Bernard de Mandeville*, VI, 151-5)

Browning is consciously gathering together his life's interests, and is linking them all together with the bond of poetry. Poetry is Browning's means of communicating knowledge through love; it is his means of redeeming the time; it is his incarnation of thought into the palpable line.

The sub-title of the last book of poems, *Asolando* (1889) is, suitably enough, *Fancies and Facts*, and again the *Prologue* introduces the still-inspiring influence of Elizabeth, leaving Browning's view of nature "palpable fire-clothed." Immediately the poet is reminded of the experience of Moses before the burning bush when God revealed his nature as "I am." God's mode of being transcends the poet's mode, although again there is an analogy between what the poet has created and God's supreme acts in creation and redemption. Love is still the means of capturing the eternal and sharing the being of God:

> . . . condense
> In a rapture of rage, for perfection's endowment,
> Thought and feeling and soul and sense—
> Merged in a moment which gives me at last
> You around me for once, you beneath me, above me— . . .
> The moment eternal. . . .   (*Now*, 4-12)

That is the core of the *Now*, and it is also the *Summum Bonum*. Browning has returned to the style of the earlier love lyrics with a new-found freshness and spontaneity that cannot be denied. Again in the volume we find evidence of Browning's continuing interest in the painters of the Renaissance, and the art of music as an accompaniment to love (*Beatrice Signorini*, and *Flute-Music, with an Accompaniment*). A poem somewhat reminiscent of the earlier religious monologues is *"Imperante Augusto Natus Est,"* with the same old re-examination of the impact upon the pagan world, both in the nineteenth and in the first centuries, of the birth of Christ. *Development* deals on the surface with man's literary capabilities, but with the higher criticism of Homer (and by implication, the Bible too) on a deeper level. Poetry, Browning argues, is superior to ethics for its teaching value, and it maintains the interest besides.

The *Epilogue* to *Asolando* occupies in Browning's work a similar place to *Crossing the Bar* in the poetry of Tennyson. But in Browning's poem there is an evaluation of his life's work even more pointed and perceptive than in Tennyson's poem. Life and Love and Striving are uppermost in Browning's mind at the end of his life as at the beginning. He looks still ahead to a bright future, confident with a sure and certain hope that life here is preparation for a greater life hereafter. Browning's optimism at this moment is no easier than it has ever been for him. Life is hard; faith is obscured by necessary doubt; truth is ever clouded with disguise. But man must love to exercise his highest power, thereby finding the meaning in his striving. The pattern of Browning's life is as complete as his art and conscience can make it, and it is a continuous whole, consistent, meaningful, when seen as a pattern of dominant themes linked by an informing thread. We recall the last lines of *Pauline*:

> And, though this weak soul sink and darkness whelm,
> Some little word shall light it, raise aloft,
> To where I clearlier see and better love,
> As I again go o'er the tracts of thought
> Like one who has a right, and I shall live
> With poets, calmer, purer still each time,
> And beauteous shapes will come for me to seize,
> And unknown secrets will be trusted me
> Which were denied the waverer once; but now
> I shall be priest and prophet as of old.
>
> Sun-treader, I believe in God and truth
> And love; . . . .   (1010–21)

God, truth, and love, painted on the banner of the Incarnation, accompanied all of Browning's poetry, and gave him that optimism which was so costly a prize:

"Strive and thrive!" cry "Speed,—fight on, fare ever There as here!"

Time ceased for him, and place became the abstraction of "there." Browning passed to the enjoyment of the total vision of which, in life, he had caught a glimpse of the arc.

Because of his many attempts to define the exact nature of faith and belief, revelation and love, time and Incarnation, Browning is unsatisfying to many readers; to many critics the poetry can be viewed finally as only a series of attempts to explain insurmountable paradoxes. Thus such a perceptive critic as F. R. G. Duckworth, in a book which ushered in a new approach to Browning, *Browning, Background and Conflict*, finds in the poet a conflict between two points of view—that reality is something timeless, or reality is an endless series in time: "The difficulties inherent in the conception of a timeless and spaceless Absolute are as old as the idealist philosophy itself, and have never yet been solved in a way which carried general conviction. If Browning arrived at some solution satisfactory to himself, it is not anywhere expressed in his poems" (161). Surely Duckworth has almost unwittingly hit exactly upon the crux of the matter. Just because Browning constantly returned to the old interests for a new look at them, just because he reworked the old themes and re-examined the old problems and mysteries, Browning must have felt that he had not yet reached a finality. But the "solution satisfactory to himself" was that only in terms of the Incarnation could he make sense of timeless reality and temporal existence. The problem of time in Browning is not primarily a philosophic problem; instead it is a religious mystery linked indissolubly with the Incarnation. The natural mystery of human love is the starting-point in Browning of an encounter with the Incarnation. The love of man and woman is the finite manifesting itself as the shadow of the infinite. The images of human love are the only means which man can validly use in discourse about divine love. Browning has passed from the single vision of the literal text to the deeper inquiry of metaphysical thought.[3] Austin Farrer defines metaphysics as the systematic elaboration of contemplative thinking. It is just that kind of thought which is the core of the Pope's monologue. Farrer describes the complex in which such thought originates:

Whenever the mind contemplates the deep mystery of what it is to know or to love,

[3]Hoxie Neale Fairchild attributes single vision or equivocation to Browning, without noting that his discourse is analogical: "The Incarnation is the eternal identification of man and God in one spirit of loving sacrifice which is manifested in all its power whenever a good man and a good woman, like Robert and Elizabeth, are deeply in love" (*Religious Trends*, IV, 145–6).

or to be an embodied spirit, or to be subject to the form of time, and yet be able to rise above the temporal stream and to survey it: whenever we consider the vitality and the richness, the inexhaustible individuality of the being whom as wife or friend we love: when we aspire to ask of the forces of nature, not how they work simply, but what in themselves they are: when we advance from curiosity to admiration, and stand upon the brink of awe: then we are thinking in the form from which metaphysical philosophy arises.[4]

That form is Browning's habitual mode of thought. Love in Browning is, as it is with Farrer, "faith reflected into action."[5] The act of believing charity is a real supernatural effect, a part of the great mystical action, and a foretaste of the beatific vision. On earth the arc is still the arc of pure charity; we must wait until heaven for the perfect round.

Analogical discourse was one means Browning used in trying to convey something meaningful about what is unique. Already the manifold problems of language present themselves, and they become greater when Browning tries not only to express the unique, but to combine in it all of the rest of his poetical experience. Language is linear, and one must move from idea to idea. The poet cannot create a complex of thought which takes just an instant to comprehend. So our thin minds creep from thought to thought, and what is a unity becomes a succession. Language and even thinking then tend to become analytical and successive. John Locke argues that we get our concept of time from our succession of thoughts where one idea follows another. Time then is merely a product of the limitations of our mode of thought, and not a part of reality. Browning, setting himself against this English empirical tradition, argues with the philosophical realists that we are bound to time, and so our temporality, despite the belief that it is limited to this life, is a real part of it. But we experience in a space-time continuum that may be interrupted in the known course of history. The poet cannot convey the whole course of history, or the whole space-time continuum. He cannot express the wholeness of the perception which contains many things that are not thought. Hence he is limited to single vision. The simultaneous pattern becomes divided and fragmented; individual terms refer to abstract concepts, and images begin to refer to metaphysical realities. Metaphor, and then analogy are used to locate and describe deity. But the poet's perception remains a unified experience, and he has to draw out the ductile vision into connected

---

[4]*The Glass of Vision*, 77.
[5]*Ibid.*, 61.

thoughts, and end by seeing them in a flash. The reader must enter into this somewhat mystical experience to try to catch the poet's vision. He must become involved in the matter to such an extent that his experience is analogous to the poet's original synthesis. Browning tries many methods to achieve the illusion of simultaneity: parenthesis (*A Death in the Desert*), grammatical complexity and concision (*Paracelsus* and *Sordello*), multiple dialogue (the plays), and recapitulation (*The Ring and the Book*).

The problem of expressing the unique linguistically led Browning to the use of analogy, and his greatest efforts were expended in trying to define the meeting point between God and man—the supreme battleground of religion and morality. For Browning that meeting point is love. Yet love takes place in time, not as an unique experience in the total experience of mankind, but unique in the lives of the individual lovers. For the individual the love-time is the unique revelatory experience, and, in that moment, time is redeemed; history is filled with opportunity; and man is faced with choice.

Browning used many different analogies in trying to examine the mystery of love in the Incarnation—music, poetry, painting, sculpture, religion, and love itself. Music, perhaps, for its success in capturing the moment of revelation, was one of the most fruitful of Browning's analogies. From at least the time of St. Augustine (*De Trinitate*, XII.xiv. 23), music has provided an evocative method of inquiring into the nature of being. F. H. Brabant in his Bampton Lectures for 1936, *Time and Eternity in Christian Thought*, applies the analogy of music to time in history. History, like music, may be regarded as a movement culminating in an end, or as a movement that is complete and valuable as a whole. The musician is able to grasp the whole movement of a work at once. The whole form is apprehended, and that action of cognition suggests the *Totum Simul* of scholastic theology which is a part of eternity: "I would not say that in such experiences we are eternal, for in eternity such an experience would last and would cover all spheres of conscious life, but we can say that they show us an image of eternity in Time, thereby revealing that there is no impassable gulf between the two."[6] The eternal is never in the temporal as a part of it, but our apprehension of it is mediated through temporal things—by nature, by the prophets and poets, by the thoughts of our hearts, by

[6] Brabant, *Time and Eternity*, 162.

the Son who, though he shares the eternal changeless of God, yet in his incarnate life is *"Immensi Patris mensura Filius."* The glimpsing and grasping of eternity which Browning could cherish in the moment of love as an analogue of the Incarnation were really the beginning of a taste of heaven. His movement into the eternal was a suspending of temporal and spatial existence, and an enjoyment of simultaneity. Browning's heaven, put in these terms, is very close to what Baron Von Hügel describes as "Eternal Life."[7] It is in time that the future is carved out, and it is in time that heaven is prepared for. For Browning time is the battle-ground where man is tested for his ability to grow in the life to come. The Incarnation is the God-given means by which the battle in time is to be won. The reflection of eternity which we perceive on earth in Browning's terms is the arc of the perfect circle.[8] The life which is striving here is there fulfilment; it is the role of religion, and in religion the role of the Incarnation, and in the Incarnation the role of Love, to yield an experience of the arc. Von Hügel sums up in the last paragraph of his *Eternal Life* (396):

> And Religion, in its fullest development, essentially requires, not only this our little span of earthly years, but a life beyond. Neither an Eternal Life that is already achieved

[7]Von Hügel, *Eternal Life* (383):
Eternal Life, in the fullest thinkable sense, involves three things—the plenitude of all goods and of all energizings that abide; the entire self-consciousness of the Being Which constitutes, and Which is expressed by, all these goods and energizings; and the pure activity, the non-successiveness, the simultaneity, of this Being in all It has, all It is. Eternal Life, in this sense, precludes not only space, not only clock-time—that artificial chain of mutually exclusive, never equal moments, but even *duration*, time as actually experienced by man, with its overlapping, interpenetrating successive stages.

[8]Von Hügel elaborates the same connections between time and eternity that we have seen in Browning:
Time then, in the sense of *duration* (with the spiritual intercourse and the growth in spiritual character which we develop and consolidate in such time), is, for us men, not a barrier against Eternal Life, but the very stuff and means in and by which we virtually experience and apprehend that Life. Man's temporal life is thus neither a theory nor even a vision; nor something that automatically unrolls itself. Nor, on the other hand, is it, even at its deepest, itself the Ultimate experienced by man. But man's life is one long, variously deep and wide, rich and close, tissue of (ever more or less volitional) acts and habits—instinctive, rational, emotive; of strivings, shrinkings, friction, conflict, suffering, harmony, and joy; and of variously corresponding permanent effectuations in and by the spirit thus active. And thence man's life is full of cost, tension, and drama. Yet such an individual life never experiences, indeed never is constituted by, itself alone; but it is ever endlessly affected by the environment and stimulation of other realities. And the whole of this interconnected realm of spirits is upheld, penetrated, stimulated, and articulated by the one Infinite Spirit, God. Thus a real succession, real efforts, and the continuous sense of limitation and inadequacy are the very means in and through which man apprehends increasingly (if he only thus loves and wills) the contrasting yet sustaining Simultaneity, Infinity, and pure Action of the Eternal Life of God. (*Eternal Life*, 386-7.)

here below, nor an Eternal Life to be begun and known solely in the beyond, satisfies these requirements. But only an Eternal Life already begun and truly known in part here, though fully to be achieved and completely to be understood hereafter, corresponds to the deepest longings of man's spirit as touched by the prevenient Spirit, God. . . .

Because Browning gave profound expression to these thoughts, men could see him as a great religious poet.[9] The fact remains that a much greater amount of Browning's poetry than the obviously religious has a firm basis in religious faith. Some of Browning's contemporaries perceived the breadth of Browning's achievement, but none seemed to realize that there was a unity in the poetic activity which could hold seemingly antagonistic elements together in a composite whole. The Incarnation of Christ provides that unifying bond. Dean Inge realized the enormous contribution which the poets had made to the theological climate when he declared that "the poets have been our most influential prophets and preachers in the nineteenth century."[10] Others, like Hastings Rashdall,[11] T. H. Green,[12] Bishop Wordsworth, and Archbishop William Temple[13] also testified to the same sentiment. Now, in

[9]It is not surprising that Von Hügel had a great admiration for Browning, since he found in the poet the complexities of life and the profundity of thought that he most enjoyed. *Eternal Life* (of which the Baron tells us, "I wrote the thing praying; read it as written, Child!") is astonishingly close to Browning in many of the conclusions that it reaches. The "Child," Von Hügel's niece, Gwendolen Greene, writes in her "Introduction" to his letters to her: "He loved Browning. He loved Browning very much, and used to read him aloud to me in the garden at Clonboy." And in the letters there is a reference to "Browning's great *Ring and the Book*" of which Von Hügel "had not realized the very happy fact that you knew it well already." (*Letters from Baron Friederich Von Hügel to a Niece*, ed. Gwendolen Greene [Chicago: Regnery, 1955], 19, 92, 103, 133)

[10]Dean Inge, from *Studies of English Mystics*, as quoted in Elliott-Binns, *English Thought*, 296.

[11]". . . It was the opinion of Hastings Rashdall, for example, that 'Tennyson and Browning were the greatest theological teachers of their generation'; and, going further back, we have the confession of Robertson Smith that the impression made upon him by *Ecce Homo* was nothing like so deep as that made by *Christmas Eve and Easter Day*" (Matheson, *Life of Hastings Rashdall*, 177; Black and Chrystal, *William Robertson Smith*, 535; as quoted in Elliott-Binns, *English Thought*, 296).

[12]"A reason was put forward in the introduction by T. H. Green to *Prolegomena to Ethics* (1869) when he said that in such works as *In Memoriam* and *Rabbi Ben Ezra* 'many thoughtful men find the expression of their deepest convictions'" (*Ibid.*, 296).

[13]*Ibid.* (198–9): "It is, however, probable, that great as was the influence of Tennyson, that of Browning was even greater. At the beginning of our period Oxford was already taking him very seriously and the abler under-graduates analysed his poems, corresponded about their different interpretations, and discussed his writings in essay clubs. Browning, it need hardly be said, was no trained theologian; but he had a wide and comprehensive knowledge of the Bible and had penetrated into some by-ways of religion and theology which were little known to the theologians of his day. He had also a remarkable insight into the minds of the writers of the Scriptures and of those whom they portray. This can be seen with regard to the Old Testament in 'Saul', and in regard to the New in 'A Death in the Desert', which William Temple describes as the

the present resurgence of Browning studies in examinations of Victorian poetry, it would be wise to be creative rather than destructive; it would be wise to seek for poetic principles like harmony, unity, wholeness of vision, rather than fragmentation, duality, and conflict. It may be that the Incarnation is just one of several means which Browning used to unify poetic experience. For all of his life it seemed to be the controlling means:

> My God, my God, let me once look on thee
> As though naught else existed, we alone!
> And as creation crumbles, my soul's spark
> Expands till I can say,—Even from myself
> I need thee and I feel thee and I love thee.
>
> *Pauline* (1833)

> I have faith such end shall be:
>   From the first, Power was—I knew.
> Life has made clear to me
>   That, strive but for closer view,
> Love were as plain to see.
>
> When see? When there dawns a day,
>   If not on the homely earth,
> Then yonder, worlds away,
>   Where the strange and new have birth,
> And Power comes full in play.
>
> *Reverie* (*Asolando*, 1889)

best commentary on the fourth Gospel (in *Foundations*, 216, note 1). One of his greatest merits was an insistence on the inadequacy and relativity of natural science, and the need to take further account of the affections and their intuitions. He had also a faculty for applying the teachings of Christianity to the conditions of the time."

BIBLIOGRAPHICAL NOTE

Students of Browning's religion should examine the theistic prejudices of Mrs. Orr ("Religious Opinions of Robert Browning" [1891]) and the influential attack of Henry Jones (*Browning as a Philosophical and Religious Teacher*, 1891) by consulting Hugh Martin's *The Faith of Robert Browning* (1963) and Philip Drew's "Henry Jones on Browning's Optimism" (*Victorian Poetry*, II [1964], 29–41). Jones stresses the conflict between Browning's certain optimism and his intellectual agnosticism: how then can man know that God manifests himself in man? Drew attacks Jones's method, a distorted pastiche of quotation and questionable interpretation from a few non-dramatic poems, and also his supposition that Browning elaborated a systematic philosophy capable of refutation. Santayana ("The Poetry of Barbarism," [1900]) condemns Browning's basing his Christianity upon personal experience rather than reason and revelation. E. D. H. Johnson (*The Alien Vision of Victorian Poetry*, 1952) argues further that Browning's anti-intellectualism derives from the Romantics. Seeking to answer Jones, Santayana, and Johnson, Norton B. Crowell (*The Triple Soul: Browning's Theory of Knowledge*, 1963) tries to redeem Browning's epistemology by relating it to his religious beliefs and moral values.

General treatments of Browning's beliefs are found in C. R. Tracy ("Browning's Heresies," *Studies in Philology*, XXXIII [1936], 610–25) and J. W. Cunliffe ("Browning's Idealism," *Transactions of the Wisconsin Academy*, XVII [1913], 661–81). Tracy shows that Browning's emotional faith, with its intellectual content eaten away by doubt, is "an off-shoot of his theory of love decked out in philosophical jargon." H. B. Charlton ("Browning as a Poet of Religion," *Bulletin of the John Rylands Library*, XXVII [1943], 271–306) finds Browning more orthodox, and first suggests the relationships between poems on love and art and the religious themes that we shall examine. To Joseph E. Baker, supporting Tracy against Charlton, Browning the Romantic worships Nature in the form of sexual energy, endowed by him with the Christian attributes of divine benevolence ("Religious Implications in Browning's Poetry," *Philological Quarterly*, XXXVI [1957], 436–52).

More specialized studies include J. W. Harper's biographical and historical analysis, "Browning and the Evangelical Tradition" (*Dissertation Abstracts*, XXI [1961], 3089–90); W. O. Raymond's "Browning and Higher Criticism" (*PMLA*, XLIV [1929], 590–621; reprinted in *The Infinite Moment*, 1950, 19–51); F. E. L. Priestley's inquiry into a reticent Browning's beliefs about God and immortality in "A Reading of *La Saisiaz*" (*University of Toronto Quarterly*, XXV [1955], 47–59); and Boyd Litzinger's appraisal of Browning's attitude towards the Roman Catholic Church and churchmen in "Robert Browning and the Babylonian Woman" (*Baylor Browning Interests*, No. 19 [1962]).

A summary of three critical schools on Browning's religion is made in Kingsbury Badger's " 'See the Christ stand!' " (*Brown University Studies in English*, I [1955], 53–73): Browning is a reactionary driven by contemporary scepticism back to orthodoxy (Phelps, DeVane, Betty Miller), a liberal tending towards Theism (Mrs. Orr, Moncure Conway, Josiah Royce), or an ordinary, confused, vague believer, tinged with variously-interpreted heresies (Santayana, Duckworth, Fairchild). There are three reasons for these different views: difficulty in assessing complex Victorian intellectual conflicts, Browning's free and ambiguous use of theological terminology, and his response to Higher Criticism. Badger concludes that Browning's faith was grounded in his experience of God as Love, rather than in historical events, the Bible, or the creeds, however they were presented or attacked. Just how Browning expressed his experience of God as Love in his poetry is the theme of this book.

SELECT BIBLIOGRAPHY

Browning, Robert. *The Works of Robert Browning*. Ed. with introductions by F. G. Kenyon. London: Smith, Elder, 1912. Centenary Edition, ten volumes.

—— *Dearest Isa* [Correspondence with Isabella Blagden, 1861–1872]. Ed. E. C. McAleer. Austin: University of Texas Press, 1951.

—— *Letters of Robert Browning Collected by Thomas J. Wise*. Ed. Thurman L. Hood. London: Murray, 1933.

Berenson, Bernard. *Aesthetics and History*. New York: Doubleday Anchor, 1954. First edition, 1948.

Brabant, F. H. *Time and Eternity in Christian Thought*. London: Longmans, 1937.

Charlton, H. B. "Browning as a Poet of Religion," *Bulletin of the John Rylands Library*, 27 (1942–3), 271–306.

Cook, A. K. *A Commentary upon Browning's "The Ring and the Book."* Oxford: University Press, 1920.

Cullmann, Oscar. *Christ and Time*. Tr. Floyd V. Wilson. London: S.C.M. Press, 1951.

DeReul, P. "Browning on Art, Religion, and Science," *Publications of the Rice Institute*, 13 (1926), 280–304.

DeVane, William C. *Browning's Parleyings: The Autobiography of a Mind*. New Haven: Yale University Press, 1927.

—— *A Browning Handbook*. New York: Appleton-Century-Crofts, 1955.

—— "The Virgin and the Dragon," *Yale Review* (September 1947), 33–46.

Duckworth, F. R. G. *Browning, Background and Conflict*. London: Benn [1931].

Duffin, H. C. *Amphibian*. [London:] Bowes and Bowes [1956].

Elliott-Binns, L. E. *English Thought, 1860–1900; The Theological Aspect*. London: Longmans, Green, 1956.

Fairchild, Hoxie Neale. *Religious Trends in English Poetry*, volume IV (1830–1880). New York: Columbia University Press, 1957.

Farrer, Austin. *The Glass of Vision*. The Bampton Lectures for 1948. Westminster: Dacre Press, 1958.

Faverty, F. E. *The Victorian Poets: A Guide to Research*. Cambridge, Mass.: Harvard University Press, 1956.

Gest, John Marshall. *The Old Yellow Book*. Boston: Chapman, 1925.

Gilson, Étienne. *Painting and Reality*. A. W. Mellon Lectures in the Fine Arts, 1955. New York: Meridian [1959].

Gosse, Edmund. *Robert Browning Personalia*. London: Unwin, 1890.

Griffin, N. W., and Minchin, H. C. *The Life of Robert Browning*. New York: Macmillan, 1910.

Hodell, C. W. *The Old Yellow Book*. Washington: Carnegie, 1908.

Huizinga, John. *The Waning of the Middle Ages*. New York: Doubleday Anchor, 1954. First edition, 1924.

Hutton, John A. *Guidance from Robert Browning in Matters of Faith.* Edinburgh: Oliphant, Anderson, and Ferrier, 1903.

James, Henry. "The Novel in *The Ring and the Book*," *Quarterly Review* (July 1912), 75–87.

Jones, Henry. *Browning as a Philosophical and Religious Teacher.* Glasgow: James Maclehouse, 1896.

Maritain, Jacques. *Creative Intuition in Art and Poetry.* A. W. Mellon Lectures in the Fine Arts, 1952. New York: Meridian [1959].

Marsh, John. *The Fulness of Time.* London: Nisbet, 1952.

McPeek, James A. "The Shaping of *Saul*," *Journal of English and German Philology*, 44 (1945), 360–6.

McElderry, J. B. "The Narrative Structure of Browning's *The Ring and the Book*," *Research Studies of the State College of Washington* (September 1943), 193–233.

——— "Victorian Evaluation of *The Ring and the Book*," *Research Studies of the State College of Washington* (June 1939), 75–89.

Milsand, Joseph. "La Poésie Anglaise depuis Byron," *Revue des Deux Mondes* (15 août, 1851), 661–89.

——— "La Poésie Expressive et Dramatique en Angleterre: M. Robert Browning," *Revue Contemporaine* (15 septembre, 1856), 511–46.

Orr [Alexandra], Mrs. Sutherland. *Life and Letters of Robert Browning.* Revised by Frederick G. Kenyon. Boston: Houghton Mifflin, 1908.

——— "The Religious Opinions of Robert Browning," *Contemporary Review*, 60 (December 1891), 876–91.

Pigou, A. C. *Browning as a Religious Teacher.* London: Clay, 1901.

Priestley, F. E. L. "Blougram's Apologetics," *University of Toronto Quarterly*, 15 (1945–6), 139–47.

Raymond, W. O. *The Infinite Moment.* Toronto: University of Toronto Press, 1950.

Smith, C. Willard. *Browning's Star Imagery.* Princeton: University Press, 1941.

Temple, William. "Robert Browning," in his *Religious Experience and Other Essays.* Ed. A. E. Baker. London: Clarke, 1958.

Tracy, C. R. "Bishop Blougram," *Modern Language Review*, 34 (1939), 422–5.

——— "Browning's Heresies," *Studies in Philology*, 33 (1936), 616 ff.

Von Hügel, Friedrich. *Eternal Life.* Edinburgh: Clarke, 1948.

Wiseman, Cardinal. Review of *Bishop Blougram's Apology*, *The Rambler*, 5 (January 1856), 54–71.

INDEX